Launch Pad UK

Launch Pad UK

Britain and the Cuban Missile Crisis

Jim Wilson OBE

Pen & Sword
AVIATION

First published in 2008 and reprinted in this format in 2016 by
Pen & Sword Aviation
an imprint of
Pen & Sword Books Ltd
47 Church Street, Barnsley, South Yorkshire S70 2AS

ISBN 978-1-47388-665-0

A CIP catalogue record for this book is
available from the British Library.

Typeset in 11/13pt Palatino by
Concept, Huddersfield

Printed and bound in England by
By CPI Group (UK) Ltd, Croydon, CR0 4YY

Pen & Sword Books Ltd incorporates the Imprints of Pen & Sword Aviation,
Pen & Sword Maritime, Pen & Sword Military, Wharncliffe Local History,
Pen & Sword Select, Pen & Sword Military Classics, Leo Cooper,
Remember When, Seaforth Publishing and Frontline Publishing.

For a complete list of Pen & Sword titles please contact
PEN & SWORD BOOKS LIMITED
47 Church Street, Barnsley, South Yorkshire, S70 2AS, England
E-mail: enquiries@pen-and-sword.co.uk
Website: www.pen-and-sword.co.uk

Contents

Acknowledgements

The Thor era, which saw the UK, and more particularly the East of England, turned into the West's first operational launch pad for nuclear ballistic missiles, marked a highpoint of danger in Cold War Britain. There is no doubt the missile launch pads were prime targets for the Soviet Union. The 4,000 or so RAF personnel who kept the missiles at a state of wartime readiness round the clock, minutes from firing, were under no illusions. They were aware, even if the British population as a whole was not, of the dangers of providing launch sites for American missiles. Moreover, they knew that in the final analysis it required American authority and the assistance of USAF personnel to launch Thor on its deadly mission. The story of the Thor squadrons, and of the RAF's brief missile era, has not been well recorded. The crews who kept the Thor force on constant alert comprised an élite, efficient and well-disciplined group, with high morale in spite of the long, tedious shifts, day and night and in all weathers. Their constant exercising and maintenance of peak readiness, matched only by their colleagues in the far-better-known, more glamorous V-force, came to the fore at the time of the Cuban missile crisis.

I am immensely grateful to all those former Thor personnel who have contributed their memories and recollections of what it was like to serve in the RAF's missile squadrons; how they felt about maintaining operational readiness of nuclear-tipped missiles that needed to be launched within fifteen minutes or less, if the order to fire was given; their experiences of training for their role in the United States of America; and their reactions at finding themselves on the brink of nuclear conflict during the tense days of the Cuban crisis.

The story of Thor raises many questions about the politics of the most dangerous period of the Cold War, and whether deployment of American missiles and nuclear might in the UK ensured that the British population was safer, or in truth made us a great deal more vulnerable.

I am also very grateful to those many former RAF personnel who have made available photographs recording the Thor bases, their impact on life in the East of England, and the part the RAF played in gaining experience of launching this most deadly weapon at Vandenberg Air Force Base in the United States.

My thanks also to Archant Norfolk, publishers of the *Eastern Daily Press*, for permission to use photographs from their library, and to quote extensively from contemporary *Eastern Daily Press* reports of the arrival of Thor in East Anglia, and the sometimes violent protests that the building of the launch pads evoked from the fledgling CND movement.

I hope this book is a fitting tribute to the Thor squadrons and their place in Cold War history.

Finally, my thanks to my wife for her support and assistance.

Jim Wilson OBE
Carleton Rode, Norfolk

CHAPTER 1

Britain at the Brink

Most of us who lived through the iconic 'swinging sixties' look back to the era that gave us the Beatles, the Twist, the mini-skirt, McDonald's fast food, and the rise of feminism and 'flower power', as if those years were defined by a golden age of permissiveness and of alternative culture. But the sixties had a darker side: for instance, the assassinations of America's youngest President, Jack Kennedy; of his brother and fellow politician, Robert Kennedy; and of Martin Luther King, whose powerful speech, 'I have a dream ...', so inspired the American civil rights movement.

The sixties were also the era of the Berlin Wall, which indelibly defined the Cold War. Most chilling of all, although few of us in Britain realised it at the time, the sixties saw the most dangerous days in human history, when the world stared into the abyss of nuclear war. In England, Thor nuclear-tipped ballistic missiles stood on a round-the-clock wartime state of alert ready to be fired; the nuclear version of 'light the blue touch-paper' came very close indeed to happening. These were the 'other' missiles of the Cuban missile crisis, which made Britain, in effect, America's launch pad.

Ask almost anyone of the generation that experienced the sixties what single world-shattering event from that decade dominates their memory, and nine out of ten will reply the assassination of President Kennedy. They may well recall, with remarkable clarity, where they were when they heard the news. But ask those same UK sixties survivors when they, and the rest of the world, were in greatest danger of perishing during that remarkable decade, and it is unlikely they would opt for the weekend of 27/28 October 1962. For most of us it could so very easily have been our last weekend on earth. Yet, astonishingly, the fact that Britain's nuclear deterrent forces went to an unprecedented level of readiness was kept secret from the public.

It was the era of Harold Macmillan's 'You've never had it so good', but as an old man Macmillan is said to have had recurring nightmares about the events of that weekend. The Cold War temperature was plunging fast, as Khrushchev's foreign policy provoked confrontation. The outcome was the Cuban missile crisis of 1962. In most people's minds it was an event taking place thousands of miles from UK shores. But it became so nearly the catalyst that plunged the Cold War into nuclear winter. And, if that had happened, the UK and Europe would have been as much the battle-ground as America and the Caribbean.

In this climate of perceptible tension the Western World's first ever strategic ballistic missile squadrons were formed in rural England. In the late fifties, all the way down the East of England from Yorkshire, through Lincolnshire to Norfolk, Cambridgeshire and Suffolk, villages and hamlets became host to launch pads for the deadly Thor ballistic missile. Sixty-five feet tall, when erected on their launch pads, the white-painted rockets, resplendent in RAF roundels, were tipped with 1.45-megaton nuclear warheads. Each missile carried a destructive potential a hundred times greater than the atomic bombs that had been dropped on Hiroshima and Nagasaki and had ended the Second World War fifteen years earlier.

In 1958 I was a young newspaper journalist based at the *Eastern Daily Press*'s Thetford office in Norfolk's Breckland. RAF Feltwell, the former Second World War RAF station, that was to become the first of the Western Alliance's missile launch sites, was in my patch. Extensive secrecy surrounded the deployment in the UK of the American missiles. Under the cover of the inoffensive code-name 'Project Emily', reminiscent more of a maiden aunt than of a frightening new product of weapons research, a chilling new era in nuclear warfare was introduced that would cast an ominous shadow over the Cold War years of the early sixties. The local press knew major site works were being undertaken at Feltwell in the summer and autumn of 1958. But the joint agreement between the British and US governments to base the missiles in the UK was highly sensitive on both sides of the Atlantic. At the time there was little official information being released about what was taking place at Feltwell, and at other East Anglian sites in the Feltwell missile complex. The Government knew that by building the sites on Defence Ministry land it could keep construction away from prying eyes.

There was certainly no inkling in Norfolk, or in the other counties where sites had been earmarked for launch emplacements, of a political battle going on behind the scenes. The argument that engaged both military leaders and politicians focused on whether deployment of nuclear missiles in Britain would act as a deterrent in the British national interest; or whether, in order to provide America with a first line of defence in this dangerous new phase of the arms race, it made this country more vulnerable to a Soviet first-strike attack.

Most people who lived through the sixties in the UK, not least those living closest to the missile bases, still have little idea just how close they came to being embroiled in devastating nuclear exchanges. Even most of Britain's leading politicians of the time were seemingly unaware quite how close units of the American Strategic Air Command based in this country, Britain's V-force, and the British-based Thor missiles went to the ultimate order. Secrecy was perhaps not surprising. For years the Government had kept Peter Watkins's TV programme *The War Game* off television screens, fearing that the impact on the public of the stark facts of nuclear warfare might produce panic.

The Cuban missile crisis has been extensively documented from the American perspective. President Kennedy secretly recorded the conversations that took place in the White House between him, his colleagues and officials as they wrestled with the appalling dilemmas that could have prompted nuclear war. What happened here in Britain, as British and American nuclear forces, predominantly based in the East of England, were poised at war readiness, is far less documented. So grave was the situation at the height of the crisis that there is good reason to believe Macmillan was preparing for a Cabinet meeting which would have given the order for the first stage of hiding the British Government underground. An elaborate network of bunkers had been constructed to ensure that some kind of government could survive the holocaust of nuclear attack.

For five tense Cold War years, sixty Thor missiles were maintained primed and ready, a mere fifteen minutes from firing. Through those years of uneasy peace, the rockets and their launch crews were on a round-the-clock alert behind their high security fences. If Prime Minister Harold Macmillan had pressed the button in the early 1960s it was calculated that the British nuclear punch, represented by the Thor rockets and the V-bomber force, was sufficient to kill eight million in the Soviet Union and Warsaw Pact countries, and injure a further eight million. But at what cost to a relatively small island nation? The Soviet counter-strike, whether pre-emptive or reactive, could have caused at least as many deaths and injuries in Britain. And, as we now know, Russia's missile armoury consisted mainly of those capable only of an intermediate-range strike, so inevitably the UK would have received a far graver nuclear knock-out than the Soviet Union could ever have delivered on the United States. But the crucial question – and it has never been adequately answered – was whose finger was ultimately on the Thor trigger – the British Prime Minister's, the US President's, or the military commanders' on both sides of the Atlantic?

Looking back, it remains a largely unanswered question. On every Thor base – and there were twenty of them, each housing three launch pads – it took both an RAF and an American officer to launch a missile in anger. The RAF launch controller needed to insert his key to initiate the countdown to firing. The USAF officer had to insert his key to arm the nuclear warhead. Each received his instructions through different channels: the RAF officer direct from Bomber Command Headquarters via the four Thor Wing operations rooms; the American, from Headquarters Strategic Air Command in Nebraska, via 7th Air Division, based in the UK. During the height of the Cuban missile crisis in October 1962, when the Cold War reached its most critical moments, both RAF Bomber Command and the US Strategic Air Command were poised at the highest states of readiness to which either command went during the whole Cold War period. Both were ordered to a level of war readiness unparalleled throughout forty years of Cold War tension. So how integrated were the command structures? What would have happened had America ordered a launch and the UK authorities disagreed? And how great was the danger to the British public, exposed as they were in the front line, in the event of a Soviet attack? Some commentators believe there is evidence to suggest that had the US needed to launch an air strike against Russian missiles in Cuba, President Kennedy might have been willing to absorb a Soviet nuclear assault on a NATO ally without retaliation, if it would have avoided escalation to a third world war. Might that nuclear assault have been against the Thor sites in Britain? It is a scenario made more horrifying by the fact that, outside military circles, the British people were unaware and totally unprepared.

In a footnote to his chapter on the Cuban missile crisis, Harold Macmillan's official biographer, Alastair Horne, says, 'New information now suggests that, almost incredibly, Britain did go to the brink of mobilisation, as it were, by mistake.' He explains:

On 24 October 1962, when America's Strategic Command had moved on to 'Alert', Britain's RAF Bomber Command was itself already in the midst of an 'alert and readiness' exercise completely unrelated to events in the Caribbean. As the crisis worsened, the C-in-C Bomber Command, a relatively lowly air marshal, decided to prolong and increase the alert even further. At this stage the British nuclear forces became capable of being launched within fifteen minutes, or less, on 230 targets in the Soviet Union and Warsaw Pact countries.

Horne adds significantly, 'The decision appears not even to have been referred to the Ministry of Defence; the White House was never aware of it; nor, almost certainly, was Macmillan.'

It is alarming, but it appears to be true, that on both sides of the Atlantic the authority that so nearly took the West to war in 1962 was not ultimately political, but military. In the UK the Commander-in-Chief of Bomber Command, Air Marshal Sir Kenneth 'Bing' Cross, ordered his forces to Alert Condition Three. He did so within his delegated responsibility, but without any direct consultation with the politicians. In America, Air Force General Thomas Power, the commander of the Strategic Air Command, acting on behalf of the US Joint Chiefs of Staff, without informing the White House, raised the Strategic Air Command's readiness alert from DEFCON 3 (Defense Condition 3) to an unprecedented and un-repeated DEFCON 2 – prepare for immediate action. DEFCON 1 meant war itself!

I, as a local journalist, living and working on the doorstep of Norfolk's two Thor missile sites, at Feltwell and North Pickenham, near Swaffham, and within a few miles of some of the most potent bomber bases in the country, British and American, had no more concept than the rest of the community how horrifically close events many thousands of miles away in the Caribbean were to affecting the lives of my family and the people in my neighbour-hood, let alone the rest of the UK. The facts were undoubtedly concealed from the public. It was not until three months or so after the Cuban crisis had been resolved, in February 1963, that anything emerged in the national press to even hint at how close Britain actually went to becoming a launch pad for nuclear war. A front-page report in the *Daily Mail*, headed 'When Britain went to the brink', written by the paper's defence correspondent, was the first clue the public had to what had taken place. It was the subject of furious questioning of the Prime Minister in Parliament. MPs, angry because they felt they had been kept ignorant of potentially catastrophic events, tried to learn the truth of what had happened. But Macmillan would admit no more than that certain 'precautionary steps' had been taken. Forty-five years after the event, Denis Healey, who became Labour's Defence Secretary in 1964, told me he was still horrified at what he termed the 'exceptional and quite unnecessary secrecy' surrounding the events of October 1962.

It is sobering to those of us who lived through that period that, according to documents now in the National Archives, the British Ambassador to Cuba, who might have been thought to have been right at the eye of the storm, in a confidential message to the Foreign Secretary after the crisis had passed, commented, 'If it was a nuclear war we were headed for, Cuba was perhaps a better place to be than Britain!'

CHAPTER 2

Deterrent or Danger?

In the late fifties, when inter-government discussions on Thor's deployment were first initiated, the British and American governments considered that the introduction of missiles to the UK would make a powerful contribution to Britain's nuclear deterrent. However, many in senior positions on this side of the Atlantic considered the plan to be not so much a defensive weapon for Great Britain, but more a proxy first line of defence for the United States. Could Thor, they questioned, ever be used for anything other than a first-strike, which was against British Government policy? Far from a shield protecting the British public, wasn't it a positive danger to the safety of the UK, because self-protection would demand that the Soviets eliminate Thor and its bases as a prerequisite to winning any nuclear exchange?

In America, as the decade of the fifties drew to a close, the USA had no reliable missile capable of intercontinental flight. Until it could develop such a weapon, the only way the United States could strike back swiftly at the USSR was by having forward missile sites this side of the Atlantic. So whom was Thor designed to protect, the Americans or the British? And could a missile which required both American and British assent to its firing truly be declared a part of the British nuclear deterrent?

The USAF had long maintained nuclear bombers at airfields in East Anglia. But bombers were becoming increasingly vulnerable

9

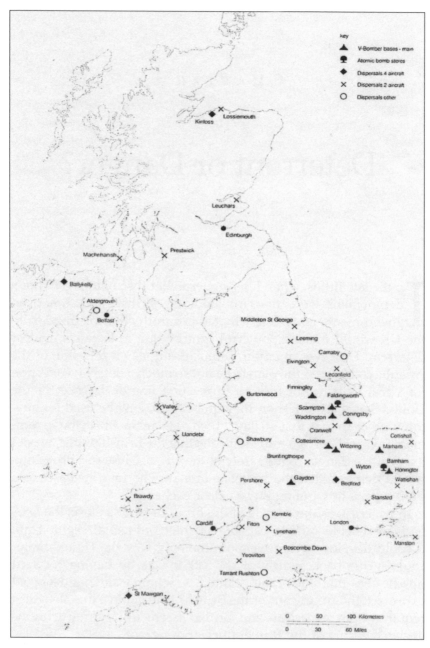

Location of V-bomber main and dispersal airfields and atomic bomb stores in February 1962.

to a pre-emptive Soviet strike. In comparison to ballistic missiles, aircraft were slow to reach their targets, and improved Soviet air defences were becoming a greater threat to them. In contrast, ballistic missiles, based along Britain's eastern corridor, could reach their targets behind the 'Iron Curtain' in a matter of minutes. But from the British public's standpoint, the formidable threat of American nuclear-armed bombers, the RAF's own V-bomber force, and the Thor launch bases, all concentrated in the East of England, made East Anglia the USSR's prime front-line target.

In early 1958, when the first Thor deployments were being planned, a note from the British Chief of Air Staff to ministers revealed deep concerns among the Chiefs of Staff over the deployment proposals. Basing Thor in the UK 'was designed to serve American ends more than British', they said. They were opposed to being rushed into a commitment to deploy. The disadvantages of the American proposals were succinctly summarised: the weapons would never be within effective British control; they were still essentially in their research and development stage; the deployment would involve the UK in a capital expense of about £10 million and an annual manpower requirement of some 4,000 men. The presence of 'these highly vulnerable missiles would make the UK a more attractive target for attack', the memorandum baldly concluded.

Early in 1958 the American Secretary of Defense, Neil McElroy, added fuel to the argument when he testified before the House of Representatives, saying that the Department of Defense should take a 'calculated risk and move faster than the testing results could in themselves justify' in preparing for the deployment of Thor and Jupiter, America's other intermediate-range rocket. In other words, deployment was the priority, even if the missile's operational capability remained unproved.

Commentators argued that Thor was more clearly a Russian first-strike target than even the Strategic Air Command bases in Britain. Logically this made sense. The Russians would have a good chance of knocking the Thor rockets out entirely on the ground, and virtually no chance of destroying them once they were launched. There was a further fear. While it might suit the United States to fight a nuclear war limited to Europe, the UK as a relatively small country geographically, and with a large population, would suffer severely, if not terminally, in an all-out nuclear conflict that enveloped Europe.

These comments mirrored similar concerns that had been expressed a decade earlier, in June 1948. At that time, scarcely two years after the last Flying Fortress of the wartime 'Mighty Eighth' Air Force took off from Honington in Suffolk, three American B59 bomber groups were allowed to return to East Anglia, to occupy bases at Marham, Lakenheath and Sculthorpe. The Cold War was intensifying, following the Communist coup in Czechoslovakia and the blockade of West Berlin. Discussions between the leaders of the USAF and the RAF recommended that at least two of these bases should be capable of accommodating aircraft armed with the atomic bomb. Buildings, aprons and loading pits for the early 'Fat Man' design of atomic weapon were installed to support possible bombing operations in Europe. Britain was in the front line of a war that, it seemed then, could break out at any moment. Yet the British Chiefs of Staff had no access to American strategic plans, despite America's nuclear clout resident on UK soil. The US/UK atomic partnership that had operated in the latter stages of the Second World War under the codename 'Tube Alloys', denoting atom bomb research and development, had abruptly ended with the passing in 1946 of the US McMahon Act. This law made it a criminal offence, subject to the gravest penalties, including death, to transmit any restricted nuclear information to another country. It left Britain, which then had no independent nuclear bomb of its own, dangerously exposed. As a forward base for American strategic bombing, the UK was likely to become the primary target of any Soviet nuclear attack. But Britain could not rely on the USAF to deal with Soviet targets that were not of direct American national interest, but might well constitute a threat to the UK. There were genuine fears that Britain could risk annihilation as a consequence of American action, without first being informed or even consulted on America's intention to launch nuclear forces from East Anglian bases. Now, in 1958, much the same dilemma faced Britain's political and military leaders with the introduction of Thor missiles.

The 1948 conundrum was resolved in December 1950 by a none-too-precise personal understanding between Truman and Attlee.

The latter had been anxious to get an agreement in writing, enshrining a principle that the United States would not consider using an atom bomb without first consulting the British Government. No formal arrangements existed at that time between the two governments controlling the use of UK bases by the USAF, only understandings worked out at senior level between the RAF and the American Third Air Division. These understandings left Ernest Bevin, the Foreign Secretary, deeply anxious about what might happen if the Americans launched a nuclear attack from British bases, particularly if the trigger was a matter that constituted no direct threat to Britain's national security.

But the Americans were adamant that there would be no written agreement. Truman told Attlee, 'It will not be in writing, since if a man's word isn't any good it isn't made any better by writing it down.' The only paragraph in the communiqué following the Attlee–Truman talks that touched upon the issue read: 'The President stated that it was his hope that world conditions would never call for use of the atomic bomb. The President told the Prime Minister that it was also his desire to keep the Prime Minister at all times informed of developments which might bring about a change in the situation.' This was a long way from the agreement Attlee wanted, which was that neither the US nor the UK would use nuclear weapons without prior consultation with each other. When Churchill regained the premiership, while he appreciated the deterrent value of the American bases in the UK, he feared the US might be provoked into a preventive or retaliatory attack from British soil, which would place this country in a highly dangerous position, or plunge it into a conflict not of our making or concern. It would be too easy for the United States to fight a nuclear war abroad, well away from its own homeland, possibly at the UK's expense.

Churchill met Truman for talks in January 1952 to seek assurances. The outcome was a memorandum that stated: 'We reaffirm that the use of these bases in an emergency would be a matter for joint decision by His Majesty's Government and the United States Government in the light of the circumstances prevailing at the time.'

The legal basis for the US military presence in Britain, and the possible consequences of its use as bases for a nuclear assault, was

to become a continuing source of controversy for British governments during the rest of the Cold War years. The 1952 Churchill–
Truman communiqué was the first and only time a framework for
the use of bases in the UK by American forces was ever set down
in black and white. Politicians and commentators have frequently
criticised its vagueness and its lack of precision. Some on the
British side thought the phrase 'a matter for joint decision' gave
the UK a veto. Most Americans felt it did no such thing and that it
was never intended to. Nevertheless, it was the basis for Thor's
deployment to the UK under joint RAF and USAF agreements.
Even as recently as 1985, when Cruise missiles were being deployed
to the UK, the Churchill–Truman communiqué remained the only
written agreement in operation. No subsequent clarifying statement about the use of British bases by American forces has ever
been made. Fundamental questions were left open. And they
became particularly pertinent as tensions racked up during the
Cuban missile crisis.

In 1957 the McMahon Act was amended to allow limited
exchanges of information between the United States and friendly
powers. Britain was the first, and in fact the only, country to
benefit. However, the fact that on British Thor bases the nuclear
warheads remained at all times in the sole control of the USAF,
and that it took a USAF officer to arm the missile's warhead,
shows how tightly the Americans insisted on retaining ultimate
control. This was a policy repeated on RAF bomber bases where
American 'Project E' nuclear weapons were made available to arm
British aircraft.

The issue clearly concerned British service chiefs in 1958. Nevertheless, the Secretary of State for Air overruled them, asserting,
without any discussion in Parliament, that the Chiefs of Staff
should not take such a negative line on the deployment of Thor.
The Government saw Thor as advantageous because Britain had
no rocket deterrent of its own. By accepting the missile bases the
UK would have a ballistic missile capability long before she could
hope to produce one herself. However, the counter-argument was
that the country was about to buy, to man and to deploy a missile
to which it could not fit its own warhead. Therefore, in no way
could it be described as an independent deterrent. Within weeks

the Cabinet authorised the project to go ahead. There was political resistance from the Labour Party, and indeed from a number of Conservative MPs, before Parliament accepted the proposal. It was at this point that introduction of the first Western ballistic missiles into the UK, the first nuclear-tipped rockets to become operational in the free-world, was given the inoffensive codename 'Project Emily' – perhaps to conceal from the public its sinister implications.

On the other side of the Atlantic the agreement was looked at in a rather different way. *Time* magazine put the US view succinctly, reducing it to an algebraic equation: 'IRBM + NATO = ICBM'. IRBM stood for intermediate-range ballistic missile, and ICBM for intercontinental ballistic missile. In common parlance it meant that America's short-term deterrent problem could be solved until the boffins could develop a true intercontinental missile.

The problem with this solution, however, was that the equation was capable of being turned on its head. What was sauce for the goose was also sauce for the gander! From the viewpoint of the Soviet Union, 'IRBM + Cuba = ICBM', capable of hitting virtually every city in the United States.

CHAPTER 3

Days of Tension

In his personal records Harold Macmillan described the weekend of 27/28 October 1962, the crucial days in the Cuban missile
crisis, as the worst two days of his life. They were without
doubt the most dangerous for all who lived through the Cold War.
Looking back, the most alarming thing is that neither public nor
Parliament was ever told how close the UK was to Armageddon.
Most people's eyes were on what was happening thousands of
miles away in the Caribbean, not what might happen to their own
lives and to their families, had the cards, played by the leaders of
East and West, fallen differently.

People watched the flickering black-and-white images on their
TV sets, from the other side of the world, of Soviet ships, laden
with nuclear missiles, approaching the US blockade thrown up
around Cuba, and thought that if war started, initially at least, it
would be fought far from British shores. In reality, in the East of
England American pilots were strapped at cockpit readiness in
their nuclear-armed aircraft. V-bombers were loaded with thermonuclear weapons and held on heightened 'Quick Reaction Alert' at
RAF bases across East Anglia and Lincolnshire. And on launch
pads down the spine of eastern England, the launch crews of
the nuclear-tipped Thor missiles were doubled in strength, and the
missiles themselves prepared for firing.

In the whole of the Second World War, British and American bomber forces dropped two million tons of bombs on Germany. It is a sobering thought that during that October weekend Bomber Command alone, through the combined efforts of the Thor force and the V-bomber force, could have delivered the nuclear equivalent of 230 million tons in a single strike – sufficient to destroy every major city and centre of population in the entire Soviet Union. By 1962 the RAF had the capability to deliver a blow equivalent to tens of millions of Second World War Lancaster bombers.

While here in Britain the population as a whole was blithely unaware of the imminent threat to its safety, those working on the Thor and V-bomber bases were in little doubt how close they were to war. Senior commanders knew that what to the outside world was passed off as an intense operational exercise was in fact an unprecedented covert state of real operational readiness.

The group captain in charge of one of the Thor complexes, housing fifteen of the sixty missiles in Britain, recalling that period some thirty years later, wrote,

> *Perhaps the worst thing was to realise that the station and dispersed sites would be hit and destroyed shortly after we had fired our own missiles, or before, if the Russians chose to make a pre-emptive strike. Although I chose not to think too much about it while the crisis was on, it was a great relief when the Air Officer Commanding Group rang to say the heat was off.*

A technician based at Feltwell in Norfolk, headquarters of the East Anglian Thor complex of launch sites, recalls the alert order bringing the Strategic Missile Force to what he describes as Readiness State Red. That meant launch crews were authorised to take their missiles to stage two hold, erect on their launch emplacements just eight minutes from lift-off. 'This was the most frightening few days of my life and an experience that will hopefully never be repeated. We were all convinced that this would be it ... it was not easy to think logically when you knew there were sixty missiles minutes from take-off.'

Former launch crew members recall the October 1962 crisis as a time of high tension. Increased levels of security were imposed, launch crews were doubled, and shift hours expanded as crews, used to routine round the clock preparedness, moved to even higher levels of alert. Probably unknown to them, and certainly kept secret from the public, the giant 185-foot dish antenna of the Jodrell Bank telescope near Manchester was temporarily handed over to the RAF to search for and track incoming Soviet missiles. The ballistic missile early-warning station at Fylingdales in York-shire did not become operational until 1963. So, at the time of the Cuban crisis, Jodrell Bank was a desperate stop-gap measure to try to gain some form of early warning of a missile attack. Given the circumstances, the response time the RAF could expect would have been minimal, a matter of minutes only.

It is as well the civilian population was unaware of what was happening under its nose. Had people realised the threat to them was so real there might have been public panic. Only the most rudimentary plans existed to protect the population, and these relied on days of prior notice if they were to be implemented effectively. It is now clear that the Home Office, the department responsible for civil protection, did nothing to activate Civil Defence plans during the Cuban crisis. In effect it hoped the threat would go away. In Norwich, downwind of several prime targets, including V-bomber bases and Thor sites, a former Civil Defence officer recalls that no steps were taken to warn the public or to initiate evacuation. During the week of highest tension, leading up to the crucial weekend of 27/28 October, there were just two meetings of the British Cabinet. At neither was there discussion of the alert states of British or American nuclear forces stationed in the UK, or of steps to protect the British public. Indeed, specifically military matters were never mentioned, despite the fact that Peter Thorneycroft, then Minister of Defence, was present at both meet-ings. Astonishingly, a meeting of the Defence Committee in the same week also made no reference to the Cuban situation.

These facts, disclosed in government records held in the National Archives, show a yawning gap between the leaders of Britain's nuclear forces and their political masters. There is little doubt that Air Marshal Sir Kenneth Cross, C-in-C Bomber Command, was acting within his devolved responsibilities in putting the Thor force and the V-force on the highest alert the RAF was ordered to throughout the Cold War years. But it is no wonder that in summing up the experience of that tense week, Cross said, 'From me downwards everything worked perfectly. From me upwards, nothing worked at all!'

CHAPTER 4

The Missile Era

The strategic missile era was a unique period for the RAF. It led to the formation of the greatest number of new squadrons ever created in peacetime. Twenty squadrons were formed, each with the suffix SM following the squadron number, denoting strategic missile, to distinguish the new units from the more traditional squadrons of the RAF. It also led to many hundreds of RAF personnel being sent to the United States to the home of the missile manufacturers, the Douglas Aircraft Company, for technical training. They studied first at the Douglas training school in Tucson, Arizona, and then took part in training launches at Vandenberg Air Force Base in California.

Inevitably the new Thor squadrons became known in service parlance as the Penguin Squadrons – 'All Flap and No Fly' – a reference to the high state of readiness they were required to maintain, and the fact that, despite continual practice countdowns, no Thor missile was ever fired from the UK.

So what was the background to Thor's entering service with the RAF?

It began relatively low-key, at the Bermuda Conference in March 1957. Anglo-American relations had reached their lowest ebb as a result of the ill-fated Suez adventure of 1956. Macmillan, who had succeeded an ailing and discredited Anthony Eden as Prime Minister, was anxious to restore relations with the United

States. Nuclear missiles, and in particular Thor, were the focus of their discussions. On 25 March 1957, the last day of the conference, Macmillan and President Eisenhower issued a joint communiqué announcing broad agreement on the deployment of Thor in the United Kingdom.

At a press conference Macmillan openly acknowledged this step would make Britain the free world's first nuclear attack target. But he added, 'We can't help that, anyway.' Under further questioning it was confirmed that the United States would be allowed to keep atomic warheads for the missiles in Britain and to attach them in the event of war. There was no mention at that stage of dual key control, nor that, as subsequently became clear, the missiles would be permanently armed. It was admitted, however, that the United States already stored nuclear bombs in England for use by Strategic Air Command bombers already stationed there. Anticipating the questions and concerns likely to be raised at home, Macmillan commented that were the missiles ever used it would mean failure of all the purposes for which they were devised. He also stressed the economic factor. The deployment would not only save Britain the cost of developing her own ballistic missile, it would strengthen the UK's deterrent at a time when financial restraint meant the UK's defence budget was under considerable strain.

Exploratory talks had been held some weeks earlier between the British Defence Minister, Duncan Sandys, and his American counterpart, Secretary of Defense Charles Wilson. Britain's own missile programme, Blue Streak, which was cancelled in 1960 for reasons of cost and vulnerability, was encountering technical difficulties.

Sandys, who had long been an advocate of missile defence, met his American opposite number to seek American aid in ballistic rocketry. He saw the opportunity of bringing the RAF into the missile age on the back of American technology.

In the House of Commons on 1 April 1957, Macmillan reported to Parliament that,

The rockets will be the property of Her Majesty's Government and manned by British troops who will receive their prior training from American experts. The rockets cannot be fired by any except the

British personnel, but the warhead will be in the control of the
United States – which is the law of the United States – and to
that extent the Americans will have a negative control; but it is
absolutely untrue to say that the President and not the British
Government will decide when these weapons will be launched and at
whom. So long as we rely upon the American warheads, and only so
long, that will remain a matter for the two governments.

It was a tricky tightrope for the British Prime Minister to walk, and
a sensitive political issue that was not going to go away during the
continuing discussions over the following months. In America one
commentator expressed the view that deploying IRBMs to the UK
made Britain vulnerable to a Soviet first strike, 'like the American
fleet tied up in Pearl Harbor'. It was fortunate, perhaps, that the
unsuspecting folk living in rural areas of Yorkshire, Lincolnshire
and East Anglia, were unaware of the controversy, or indeed the
potential targets they were to become. At this stage there had been
no public announcement of where the launch bases would be sited.

The dark shadow of possible nuclear war had hung over post-
war Britain, and particularly East Anglia, since July 1950, when
the first US nuclear weapons were deployed to the UK. At that
time, although little was publicly known about it, Norfolk and
Suffolk became hosts to some ninety sets of the non-nuclear
components of America's latest nuclear bomb. These components
were stored at USAF Strategic Air Command bases at Marham and
Sculthorpe in Norfolk, and Lakenheath in Suffolk. It was intended
that the nuclear cores – the business part of the weapons – would
be airlifted to the UK if and when an emergency was declared. But
it soon became clear this policy was unrealistic. Events could
escalate too rapidly to allow time to fly in nuclear cores from the
States. So it was decided, without any public announcement, that
the nuclear bombs in their entirety should be stored on British
bases housing American planes. Virtually all these key bases were
in East Anglia.

Meanwhile, nuclear weapons development in this country was
moving on apace. Britain's first home-manufactured operational
atomic bomb, codenamed Blue Danube, was delivered to RAF
Wittering, near Peterborough, three years later, in November 1953.

RAF Wittering was the Bomber Command Armament School. The RAF had had no experience of dealing with atomic weapons, so the BCAS was staffed with RAF personnel who had assisted in the design and development of nuclear weapons at the Atomic Weapons Research Establishment at Aldermaston. The station's operational Records Book described the arrival of Britain's first independent nuclear bombs that November as: '... marking a historic month for this unit, and indeed for the Royal Air Force and the country. During this month the first atomic bombs have been delivered to the RAF, and they are now held by this unit. These bombs will raise the striking power of Bomber Command to an order completely transcending its power hitherto.'

It was another four months, February 1954, before the public learnt of Britain's new independent nuclear strength. A statement in Parliament included the following, 'We intend as soon as possible to build up in the Royal Air Force a force of medium bombers capable of using the atomic weapon to the fullest effect ... The Royal Air Force has a major deterrent role ... Atomic weapons are in production in this country, and delivery to the forces has begun.' This statement heralded the emergence of the RAF's nuclear-armed V-bomber force.

Over the next few months, as production of the UK's own free-fall nuclear bomb was stepped up, two major nuclear bomb stores and maintenance depots were built in secret at Barnham, just outside Thetford in Norfolk, and Faldingworth in Lincolnshire. The two sites were identical in design and each covered around 23 acres. They were operated by Maintenance Command; No. 94 MU at RAF Barnham and No. 92 at Faldingworth. The principal storage buildings were divided into two for safety purposes. The larger stores held the bomb casings and their related high-explosive components. Blue Danube was a large, heavy weapon, and to facilitate handling each maintenance store was equipped with a lifting gantry at its entrance. The smaller buildings, built of solid concrete blocks, held the fissile nuclear cores in individual below ground, double combination safes. Some stores were built to hold a single plutonium core, others were intended for two cobalt cores. Each core was held for secure protection in a heavy stainless-steel drum. Barnham was built on the site of a Second World War ammunition depot, part of which was known as Barnham Little Heath, where chemical munitions were stored and filled. During the Second World War it was called No. 1 Forward Filling Depot, handling mainly mustard gas agent. The chemical weapons unit was closed and initially decontaminated in 1954. But this turned out not to be totally effective, and further remedial work was carried out in the 1990s to eliminate all traces of the chemicals used there. The nuclear storage facility that was built around the time that the chemical warfare unit closed had sufficient capacity to store sixty-four fissile cores. The number of British-manufactured nuclear weapons available to the RAF in the late 1950s and the early 1960s was fairly limited; reportedly only fifty-seven operational Blue Danube weapons were ever made, so the Barnham and Faldingworth depots were never full. Possibly part of their function was to send a message to the Soviet Union that Britain had more nuclear weapons at her disposal than was actually the case, or it may be that budgetary restrictions limited the number of bombs Britain could afford to produce independently.

Other buildings at both sites provided facilities for inspection and maintenance of the nuclear weapons. Heating and air-conditioning plant was provided to maintain a stable environment for the first generation of British bombs. By 1959 Red Beard, a new, smaller and lighter device, was coming into production, and there is evidence that these weapons and possibly others that succeeded them were stored at Barnham. The last nuclear weapons were probably removed from the site by April 1963. With the final phasing-out of the RAF deterrent in favour of submarine-based missiles, the RAF's last nuclear bombs, codenamed WE177, were removed in early 2001 from RAF Honington.

Understandably, security at the depots was extremely strict. Barnham's technical compound, known as 'Top Site', was surrounded by several high-security fences with an electric inner gate, floodlighting and observation towers. RAF police dogs and armed guards were always on duty, the dogs roaming free in a sterile area between inner and outer security fences. Electric locks to each bomb store were closely monitored from a central control building. Barnham held more than sufficient nuclear capability to flatten vast swaths of Norfolk and Suffolk for miles around. But keeping the fissile cores separate from the bomb itself ensured that an accidental detonation would not result in a full-scale nuclear disaster. How risky this venture was is hard to determine. There were clearly stringent safety precautions, though it is unlikely they would have assuaged concerns locally, had the full details of what was stored there been widely known. But the Barnham area had a history of living in the shadow of ticking time-bombs, and undoubtedly the local population were not entirely unaware of the dangers lurking on their doorsteps.

These two nuclear-bomb stores, one on the Norfolk/Suffolk border and the other in Lincolnshire, were geographically located to serve the airfields in the region. But however strategically important they were, storage so close to populated areas made large numbers of unsuspecting people in Norfolk, Suffolk and Lincolnshire frighteningly vulnerable.

There were also numerous nuclear convoys passing to and fro from the two units, and between various Royal Ordinance Factories, and the Atomic Weapons Establishment at Aldermaston. Other convoys regularly supplied the V-force stations, where Supplementary Storage Areas held nuclear weapons on base ready to be loaded aboard aircraft should war seem imminent. These required routine servicing. During transport the fissile cores were placed inside shock-proof containers securely fixed to the floor of the transporting vehicle. There was real concern that these nuclear-weapons convoys should not be caught on the public roads in a violent thunderstorm. For safety reasons regulations insisted the whole convoy, with its RAF police outriders, together with a technical and safety vehicle, should be brought to a stop in the nearest lay-by until the electric storm had passed over.

There were occasions when sudden storms caused real anxiety to the personnel who were manning them. In one incident, recalled by a former RAF officer, before the convoy could be brought to a halt a bolt of lightning hit a lamp-post close to where the actual nuclear bomb transporter was being driven. The lightning strike was followed almost immediately by a sudden very violent clap of thunder. The driver of the vehicle carrying the nuclear weapons was convinced his load had exploded. He swerved to a halt in the middle of the road and was found by the escorting crew in his cab rigid with fear, dumbstruck and totally overcome by shock. It was some time before the poor chap recovered from the whole frightening experience.

Events in the Cold War were moving fast. The American ballistic missile programme was launched in earnest by the Eisenhower administration in 1953. A handpicked group of scientists and aircraft industry leaders were set up to make recommendations on the future direction of a missile programme. Known informally as the 'Teapot Committee' (no one seems to know why, but like Project Emily it had a reassuring ring to it), it concluded in February 1954 that the Soviet threat, and the perceived 'missile gap' between the opposing superpowers, was so grave that the United States was compelled to embark on a crash development programme. They were right. Three months later, on 15 May, the Soviet Union tested an intermediate rocket, firing it 630 miles down its test range at the Kapustin Yar launch site. This Soviet success quickened the pace of a new and more dangerous phase of the arms race. America knew at that stage that she was in second place in missile development. The realisation that they were playing 'catch up' was a massive incentive to US scientists and rocket technicians. The Soviet R-5 rocket was able to deliver a 300-kiloton nuclear warhead over a range of about 750 miles, putting both London and Paris within range. At the time of Suez in 1956, Khrushchev threatened both cities with nuclear strikes. It is highly probable that his threat could have been carried out.

The American President moved to plug what was then assumed to be a widening missile gap. Eisenhower issued a presidential order to develop an IRBM (intermediate-range ballistic missile) as quickly as possible. It was to be named Thor, after the Scandinavian God of Thunder. Originally America had set its sights on going to the ultimate stage of developing an intercontinental missile in one step. But the urgency of the situation that the USA faced dictated a staged path to a missile capable of intercontinental range. Brigadier-General Bernard A. Schriever was appointed to what was named the Air Force's Western Development Division, located in Los Angeles, with an original brief to build an Atlas ICBM. Later, as it became clear how urgent a response to USSR technology had become, this was amended to a 'family' of missiles, which would eventually deliver the Atlas, the Titan and the Minuteman ICBMs. On the way, in response to the urgency prompted by Soviet successes, the Thor IRBM was developed as an interim answer. But it could only be an answer if it could be based within striking distance of the USSR, and that meant placing it in the UK.

The requirement to locate Thor's launch bases in Britain dictated that Thor, together with its associated launch equipment, had to be air-transportable, using the C-124 Globemaster transport aircraft. In a decree in December 1955 President Eisenhower gave the programme highest priority. He insisted he receive monthly updates on its progress. Within weeks the Douglas Aircraft Company was selected as prime contractor, with orders to produce 120 Thor missiles by July 1959.

CHAPTER 5

Race into Space

Christmas Eve 1955 is a significant date in the history of Thor. It was the day the Douglas Aircraft Company received a valuable Christmas present in the shape of the contract to start work on designing the new intermediate-range missile. Initially the order was for 120 missiles. The urgency of America's need was underlined by a clause insisting the weapon must be operational within the space of four years, which was by mid-1959. In fact Thor had a shorter interval between contract signing and initial operational capability than any comparable weapon, a remarkable achievement – less time indeed than General Motors was taking at the time to develop and introduce a new car model.

In securing the contract Douglas had been challenged to create a management team that could pull together existing technology, skills, abilities and techniques in a remarkably short time. They certainly matched that specification, though the prototype tests were disappointing. The first test launch took place at Cape Canaveral (now Cape Kennedy) in January 1957. It failed to lift off. In fact the first four launches were failures, some resulting in spectacular explosions. No. 2 was destroyed by the range safety officer after thirty-five seconds' flight. No. 3 blew up before ignition. No. 4 flew for ninety-two seconds before breaking apart. Finally, the fifth test launch, in September 1957, was successful. Of eighteen Thor research and development firings, from January 1957 to October

1958, seven were successful, four were partially successful and seven were failures. However, the pressure to reach an operational stage was so acute that the missile was ordered into full production in November 1957, and Thor was finally declared operational in 1959.

There is a certain irony that the first ballistic missile to be sited in England, indeed the first intermediate-range missile to be deployed anywhere in the West since the German V2 of the Second World War, could trace its parentage to the German scientists who had developed Hitler's last terror weapon. Over a thousand of Hitler's *Vergeltungswaffen*, 'vengeance weapons', fell on South-East Britain in 1944, causing widespread panic and thousands of deaths. The V2 was so terrifying because it reached its target silently, without any kind of warning. It was impossible to shoot down. It sapped civilian morale in a way the blitz had never achieved. There was no realistic defence against the V2 except by air attack on their launch sites in northern France and the Low Countries. A good proportion of V2s fell short of their intended targets, causing death and injury in areas closest to their launch sites, down the east coast of England.

The V2 was 46 ft long and carried a warhead packed with 1,650 lb of explosive. It was propelled by liquid oxygen and alcohol, and could achieve a peak height of fifty or sixty miles, and a maximum range of more than 200 miles. The 1,054 V2 rockets that fell on London and eleven counties between 8 September 1944 and 27 March 1945 caused death and injury to 9,277 people. More to the point, it demonstrated the potential of a terrifying new weapon. At the height of the onslaught that Britain suffered at the hands of Hitler's 'reprisal' weapons, Churchill appointed his son-in-law, Duncan Sandys, to investigate the Fuhrer's secret weapons. The effectiveness of the V2 rocket was not lost on Sandys. And of course it was he, as Minister of Defence in Macmillan's Government, who was so impressed by America's determination to develop Thor.

At the end of the Second World War both the British and the Americans put a high priority on capturing members of Wernher von Braun's V2 team. In the USA, the Army had taken the lead in post-war missile development, with German rocket scientists working under von Braun at the Redstone Arsenal, where the Army Ballistic Missile Agency was based. For a period the US Army and the US Air Force competed in rocket development. The Army was working on the Jupiter (SM-78) IRBM, and the USAF was developing Thor as a precursor to the Atlas ICBM. In the USSR a similar team of former German scientists worked to deliver rocket-borne missiles for use by the Communist world. During Thor's development the Americans obtained as much wartime German film of the V2, its launch sequence and its launch sites as possible, much of it from British sources. Thor would be a much more sophisticated weapon. The German V2, although crude in comparison to the rocket the Americans were working on, had been the first operationally deployed terror rocket, and the American scientists knew there were lessons they could learn from it in designing a platform to carry a nuclear warhead. While the Thor contract was America's IRBM No. 1, the Redstone missile, inappropriately christened Jupiter, the bringer of jollity, was IRBM No. 2. Both required front-line launch sites. Unless they could be based and fired far from America's borders they were useless for targeting the USSR. Thor, which eventually proved the more reliable of the two rockets, ended up deployed down England's east coast. Jupiter's launch sites were eventually located in Turkey, where one squadron was based, and Italy, which hosted two squadrons. They were the only other European countries prepared to host American IRBMs.

For a time the rivalry between the Thor and Jupiter teams – between the Army and the Air Force – assumed bizarre proportions. Relations between the Western Development Division, the USAF unit overseeing missile development, and the Army Ballistic Missile Agency were strained. Incensed that the Army was meddling in an area that formerly had been its exclusive preserve, the Air Force was also concerned that the Army IRBM, which depended on many of the same manufacturers and suppliers that the Air Force needed, would impede work on the intercontinental missile. Success was urgently needed in the national interest. Some in the Air Force feared the Jupiter programme was just the opening shot in an all-out Army attack to seize the ICBM programme and take-over the future military space programme. However, in November 1956 the Secretary of Defense, Charles Wilson, delivered

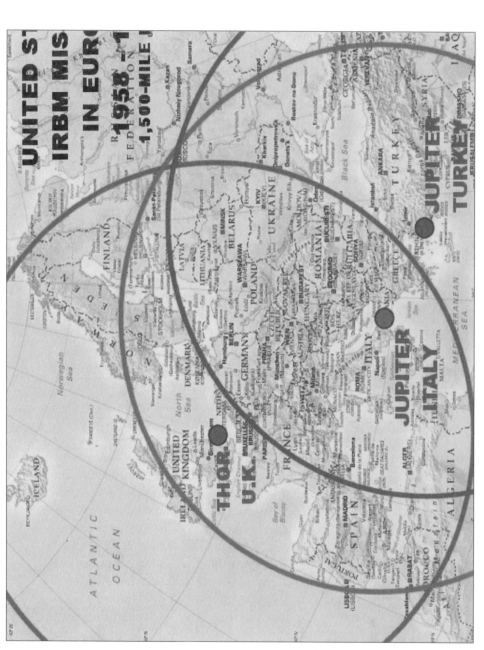

Thor and Jupiter launch sites in Europe, and their effective range.

what looked to be a body blow to the Army. He gave the Air Force sole responsibility for building and, significantly, operating all surface-launched missiles with a range in excess of 200 miles.

That meant the Army would never operate the missile it was building. But with the prospect of the Jupiter programme being cancelled, the flamboyant Major-General John Medaris argued his case forcefully with the Government, pointing out that in contrast to Jupiter's successful test flights, the Air Force had yet to fly a single missile. As a result, Jupiter survived, but under the stricture that if it succeeded the Army would not be allowed to deploy it operationally. That responsibility would still go to the Air Force. The competition between Thor and Jupiter reached almost fever pitch towards the end of 1957, as the time approached to select one or other for full production. Each side used every opportunity to discredit the other in Congressional debates and in the media. But the inter-service rivalry was brought to a sudden end with the shattering announcements which came from the Soviet Union in October 1957. The news that the USSR had become the first to launch a man-made satellite caused a profound convulsion in American society, in a way comparable to the impact 9/11 had on the nation over forty years later. People in the United States realised for the first time that the Soviet Union had the means to bring nuclear war to their own territory. War was no longer something that happened abroad. The acrimonious inter-service debate became irrelevant. President Eisenhower ordered that both Thor and Jupiter should be built. Two IRBMs, both with a requirement for European launch pads in order to be effective deterrents for America, led inevitably to agreements to deploy. And that meant a threatening presence on Russia's doorstep.

Perhaps it is no wonder that the Soviet Union was deeply alarmed by America's dispersed missiles; and that Khrushchev, in October 1962, conceived his plan to confront threat with threat, and base his own intermediate missiles at America's backdoor in Cuba. It is said the Soviet leader had the habit of greeting visitors to his Black Sea dacha by handing them a pair of binoculars and telling them to look towards the south. 'What do you see?' he would ask. When they replied nothing but sea and sky, he would take the binoculars back and, putting them to his own eyes, would bellow,

'I see American missiles in Turkey targeted at my dacha.' But the Russians were achieving marked success in missile development too.

America's dash to catch up with Soviet missile success, and close what the American military perceived was a widening missile gap, led to a scientific programme that dwarfed the historic Manhattan project, the United States effort, towards the end of the Second World War, to build and deliver an atomic bomb. Put in charge of the missile project was a tall, soft-spoken, German-born Air Force officer by the name of Bernard Schriever. Schriever had been a bomber pilot and maintenance officer during the war. He was an ardent proponent of new technology, and he headed an organisation which had a goal, in terms of scientific difficulty, spending, number of employees and, most significant of all, urgency, which overshadowed the historic project to build the first A-bomb. The scientists working on America's first atom bomb knew that neither Germany nor Japan had the ability to beat them. In contrast, there was strong intelligence to show that the Soviet Union was further ahead than America in rocket technology. Side by side with the USSR's success in building atomic and hydrogen bombs, the prospect of nuclear-tipped ballistic missiles posed a potent threat to America. During 1957 and 1958 the Soviets would have been able, had they wished, to mount a bolt-from-the-blue attack on the US mainland. Although the Soviet missile arsenal was relatively small, ballistic missiles fired from the Soviet Union would have been quite capable of hitting targets half a world away in less than thirty minutes. No US radars were then deployed that could have seen them coming, and there would have been no time for US aircraft to get airborne and escape. It would have taken US Strategic Air Command bombers operating from bases within the USA five to six hours' flying time to reach their targets in the USSR and strike back. In truth, it was a time of maximum vulnerability for the West.

General Schriever put in place a risky, but ultimately successful, system of concurrent development, production and operations. It spawned a management style later to become known as 'systems management', a concept that was widely adopted in industry. Within a relatively short time he was employing 18,000 scientists, seventeen prime and 200 sub-contractors and thousands of suppliers, to build components for a range of missiles. The major objective was to develop an intercontinental missile, Atlas. But this programme was subject to delays and fraught with difficulties, which was why, alongside Atlas, work proceeded on Thor as the urgent stop-gap. Both Atlas and Thor were liquid fuelled, fed by a combination of kerosene-like RP-1 fuel and LOX (liquid oxygen).

Thor was a direct spin-off from the Atlas programme, but once rivalries were put on one side, with significant technological help from the von Braun Jupiter programme. The first launch of Atlas took place at Cape Canaveral on 11 June 1957. An engine failed, sending it wildly off course, and it had to be blown up by the range safety officer. It was December before a successful launch was achieved, but by then the Soviets had demonstrated to the world, through the launch of Sputniks 1 and 2, how far ahead they were moving technically. It was painfully clear that a Russian rocket, capable of putting a satellite in orbit round the earth, could also propel a nuclear warhead to the United States. As if to emphasise the point, operational rockets with their warheads attached rolled through Moscow's Red Square as part of the Soviet Revolutionary Celebrations in November 1957. Hence the urgency of Thor, and the necessity for an agreement to base it in the United Kingdom, as America's only realistic response, should the Cold War drop to freezing-point. While Thor was a stop-gap, and Atlas at that stage by no means an assured success, America put into place the development of a series of follow-on rockets, in the shape of Titan and Minuteman. Thor reached initial operating capability in 1958, Atlas the following year, and both Titan and Minuteman in 1962.

Rockets, powered by dangerous and explosive liquid fuels and oxidisers, were difficult to handle. They had to be filled with these chemicals before firing, a hazardous procedure which took up valuable time. During Thor's five years' operational stand-by on its Eastern England bases, much effort was put into shortening the time it took to launch by speeding up the fuelling process. The RAF improved the launch sequence considerably, but the drawbacks of liquid fuel remained. There was little doubt that solid propellants would define the next generation of intercontinental rockets, and Minuteman saw the start of this transition to a much more sophisticated three-stage solid-propellant rocket.

Thor used many existing components, including the rocket motor developed for the Jupiter missile, and an inertial guidance unit and re-entry vehicle designed for the Atlas rocket. Sixty-five feet long and 8 ft in diameter, with a blunt nose, it was considered one of the most distinctive-looking missiles ever developed by the USA. Jupiter was slightly smaller at 60 ft tall, but it had a diameter of 9 ft. It could carry a 1,500 lb payload, the same as Thor, but its range was slightly shorter than its rival. Both missiles used the same powerplant, a Rocketdyne engine developed for the Atlas programme, and both used an all-inertial guidance navigation system. Thor was designed for use mainly against strategic targets. Its high-yield 1.45-megaton thermonuclear warhead made it an effective weapon for destroying cities, but the relatively low accuracy of its guidance system prevented it from being effective against anything but a soft target. It could never be relied upon for total pinpoint accuracy.

Thor had a range of between 1,500 and 1,725 miles. Its single-stage rocket engine, the Rocketdyne S-3d, developed 152,000 lb thrust at launch. Directional control of the missile was provided by mounting the rocket motor on gimbals and rotating it to direct the thrust. Two 1,000 lb static-thrust Vernier rockets, attached at opposite sides of the base of Thor, assisted with directional control by making minor adjustments to the missile's trajectory. These engines burnt the same fuel as the main engine. A full two-thirds of the Thor's near-65 ft casing held the liquid fuel. Thor's all-up weight was 110,000 lb, and 98,500 lb of that was the liquid fuel. Once launched, the rocket had a maximum speed of 10,250 mph and reached a height of 390 miles.

Sectional diagram of the intermediate-range Thor missile.

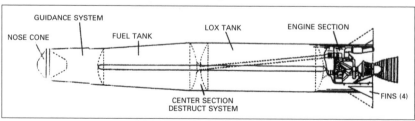

The single warhead was carried in an Atlas re-entry vehicle. The whole system was navigated by an inertial navigation system using liquid-floated gyroscopes. The linked gyroscopes detected changes in acceleration, enabling them to monitor the missile's precise location, and allowing adjustments to be made to its course. This guidance system gave the warhead a circular probability of error of some two miles on impact at maximum range, hardly a pinpoint attack, but the ferocity of its nuclear explosion would more than compensate for its lack of accuracy. For about thirteen minutes after launch the automatic pilot was controlled by a pre-set programme. Then for about a minute the auto-pilot received instructions from the AC Spark Plug inertial navigation system, which controlled the missile's flight path until the motors cut out. The nose cone, containing the warhead, then separated from the main body of the missile, the height and speed at which this occurred being governed by the range of the target from the rocket's launch point.

Thor was regarded as an effective weapon to deploy against major centres of population, airfield complexes or large military installations. Its range meant that Moscow could be hit from a launch site in the UK some eighteen minutes after the order to fire.

But Thor had two drawbacks – the time it took to pump fuel and LOX into its tanks as it went through its launch phases, and the fact that it could not be silo-launched from a protected and sub-terranean bunker. Pre-launch, the missile was kept inside a shelter on a transportable cradle. Electrical power was constantly fed to the missile to keep the gyros in the inertial guidance system in a state of readiness. The state of the missile had to be constantly monitored from instruments in its nearby launch trailers. When a

The flight profile of a typical Thor mission.

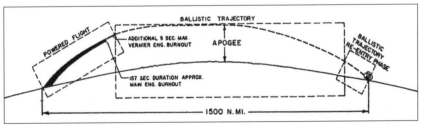

countdown was initiated, either for practice or operational reasons, an automatic sequence of events was put in train during which the shelter slid aside on tracks and the missile was erected and fuelled.

As early as February 1957, before even test launches took place, General Schriever declared that in his view about 90% of the developments in the ballistic missile programme could be applied not just to offensive capability, but also to advancing space research, and to the fledgling satellite projects. He considered ballistic missiles as a step in a process leading to flights to the moon and space travel. In retrospect, he saw his contribution to the space programme as being far more satisfying and significant than the creation of the ICBM and IRBM fleet.

As far as Thor was concerned, after it had been superseded by more powerful intercontinental-range rockets and had been withdrawn from front-line service in Britain, it went on to be used in space launches, either as a single-stage booster or in combination with various upper stages for the Telstar, Pioneer and Discoverer programmes. Thor's final military chapter was as an anti-satellite weapon. In February 1962 the USAF started a programme to provide the capability to destroy enemy spy-satellites. Unarmed tests of Thor rockets as anti-satellite missiles (ASAT) began in February 1964, and by September Thor was declared operational in this role. From then until December 1972 the USAF Air Defence Command always had two Thors on 24-hour ASAT alert.

CHAPTER 6

'Snooping' to Survive

During the Cold War intelligence was a vital tool to guarantee preparedness. To know what your opponent was capable of was to be forewarned. This was particularly true in the early and mid-1950s, when each side of the Cold War divide was determined to out-manoeuvre the other in developing nuclear weapons and ballistic missiles. Before the era of spy-satellites the only way to gather information on missile-testing and air-defence capabilities was through covert surveillance flights over the opposition's territory. Some of these highly secret and dangerous missions were flown from East Anglian airbases by both American and British crews. The information they brought back eventually led to crucial decisions to counter the Soviet threat – decisions like the joint US/UK agreement on the deployment of Thor, and the decision to turn many disused airfields from the Second World War scattered down England's east coast into missile launch sites.

The Cold War saw significant covert operations flown from airfields in East Anglia and the East of England. Details of some, but certainly not all these highly dangerous missions, have filtered out, but it is safe to say that much of what took place is still classified and remains in the archives of the Pentagon and the Ministry of Defence.

As early as spring 1951 the RAF formed a highly secret 'Special-Duty Flight' consisting of three hand-picked aircrews led by Sqn

Ldr John Crampton DFC AFC. Many of the details of this unit remain classified, but some details of what they achieved have come out through American sources. The covert RAF flight crews were trained at Barksdale Air Force Base in Louisiana, under the guise of undertaking British–American air refuelling trials. In the early months of 1951 the British aircrews learnt to operate North American RB-45C four-jet reconnaissance aircraft. In the autumn they returned to Sculthorpe in Norfolk, then a USAF base, with not three but four American aircraft, one to be used as a spare. In the following weeks they liaised at the highest levels within the Air Ministry and the Government, and worked alongside the USAF squadron of RB-45C aircraft based at the huge airbase in North Norfolk. In approving these first British spy-flights, Churchill, then Prime Minister, took a considerable political risk. In the political climate of the time, with many in the Labour Party sympathetic to Britain's former wartime ally, if any RAF over-flights of the Soviet Union and its satellites had been brought down, there would have been a real risk that it could have led to Churchill's own downfall.

The first mission was a test flight over East Germany and Berlin on 21 March 1952, partly to measure the reaction of Soviet air defences. The next venture was much more ambitious and involved considerable risks. On the night of 17 April, maintaining absolute radio silence, three RB-45C aircraft displaying RAF roundels took off from Sculthorpe. Had one of the aircraft been shot down or captured, the USA would have denied all knowledge, while the RAF would have indicated that it possessed no such aircraft. They were refuelled *en route* to the north of Denmark, and each entered Eastern Bloc air space at a predetermined time but at very different locations. One flew a northerly track that took it across the Baltic states. Another over-flew Poland and Byelorussia to spy on airfields around Minsk and the infrastructure supporting the armoured divisions of the Red Army. The third flew a course that took it over East Germany, Czechoslovakia and parts of the Ukraine all the way to the Russian border at Kharkov. Flying at night at 36,000 feet without lights, and maintaining absolute radio silence, all intelligence collection was via radarscope images, 35 mm photographs taken from the aircraft's radar display when targets were spotted. Of particular interest were Russian ballistic-missile sites.

Between them the three aircraft brought back to Norfolk images of 126 intelligence targets. Inevitably the Soviet air defence system detected the intruders. The RAF crews listened in to Soviet communications, gaining important information on their opponents' air defence capability. Soviet fighters were scrambled into the night sky, but none succeeded in homing in on any of the British-manned aircraft. Zig-zag courses were chosen to trigger as many Soviet ground radars as possible. At that time Soviet interceptor aircraft did not carry airborne radar, and all three spy-planes returned safely to Norfolk. Among installations the three missions identified were Soviet long-range bomber bases, the bases the USSR would have used to mount a strike on the UK. The information brought back by the RAF crews was crucial.

The Special-Duty Flight disbanded temporarily, but was re-formed at Sculthorpe in October 1952. Training began for a second series of over-flight missions. But in early December the plans were cancelled for political reasons. Later that month the four aircraft of the covert RAF unit flew back to the United States. At Lockbourne Air Force Base in Ohio, where they touched down, USAF personnel were stunned to see American planes displaying full RAF livery.

However, that was not the end of the story. Sculthorpe became the departure point for further spy-missions two years later, in April 1954. Further vital intelligence was gathered over much the same areas as had been the subject of the 1952 missions. On this occasion the flight plans charted three courses over USSR territory – a northern route, a central route, and a long southern route. Once again the primary targets were the Soviet long-range bomber bases. The aircraft, piloted by Sqn Ldr Crampton, taking the southern run, deep into Russian territory, ran into heavy and accurate flak approaching Kiev. Crampton was briefed to cut the mission short if there was a danger of the flight being compromised. He was unable to discard his empty wingtip tanks, which would have given him extra speed, for fear of leaving behind unmistakeable evidence for the Russians to exploit. In the event he made it safely across a thousand miles of hostile air space to the border with West Germany, where he met up with his refuelling tanker, but there were problems with the refuelling boom. Suspecting flak damage, Crampton landed near Munich to refuel before returning to Norfolk. The other two crews were luckier and returned as planned to Sculthorpe, though the Soviet air defences scrambled fighters to seek them out. In May the RAF Special-Duty Flight was finally disbanded at its Norfolk base.

Meanwhile, in August 1953 a daring daytime mission was flown by an RAF Canberra. The significance of this trip can hardly be exaggerated. The crew brought back the first glimpse that the Americans and British had seen of Kapustin Yar, the secret Soviet rocket-testing range east of Stalingrad. Intelligence reports had identified unusual activity in that area, and radio intercepts pointed to a test range in active use. There had been stories circulating that German scientists, who had worked on the V2 programme during the war and had subsequently been captured by the Russians, had been assisting with a major rocket programme. The RAF agreed to take a look during a hazardous daylight mission, which would provide the possibility of direct photography. The mission was planned in the full knowledge that it ran a very real risk of interception by Russian MiG fighters. The flight was tracked by Soviet radar as the Canberra, which had been stripped of all unnecessary equipment to reduce its weight, flew at 48,000 feet across East Germany and past Kiev. Over Stalingrad, as the crew were taking photographs of the rocket-testing range, the Canberra was attacked by Soviet fighters. Damage to the aircraft adversely affected some of the reconnaissance photography, but the Canberra survived, turned south, and followed the Volga River to the Caspian Sea, landing safely in Iran.

Some seven years later a Soviet defector, who had been involved in air defence operations, spoke of the confusion which had surrounded attempts to intercept the Canberra. In one region the air defence operator mistakenly sent fighters west instead of east. In another the Soviet interceptors ended up firing at each other. The whole episode led to a major inquiry, and many high-ranking Soviet officers were removed, purged or sent to punishment battalions. In the UK, Bomber Command's scientists went to work on the cameras that filmed radarscope images to improve night reconnaissance. The option of daytime over-flights was becoming far too risky. The product of RAF spy-flights was interpreted at the RAF's Central Reconnaissance Establishment at Brampton in Huntingdonshire. And a neighbouring RAF base, also in Huntingdonshire, RAF Wyton, was the centre for signals and electronic intelligence-gathering flights along the periphery of Soviet air space. Similarly, air-sampling missions were routinely undertaken to 'sniff' out evidence of Soviet nuclear tests and bring back information from which details of the size, type of weapon, and its capabilities could be deduced. In July 1960 an RB-47 operating from Brize Norton was shot down over the Barents Sea, which caused the Macmillan Government acute international embarrassment.

The American Air Force continued spy-flights from the UK, using Fairford as a 'take-off' point and Mildenhall as the base for refuelling tankers. By 1956 the U2 spy-plane, capable of operating above 70,000 feet, where initially it was invulnerable to Soviet air defences, took over the task of intelligence gathering. But as the United States was to find out with the shooting down of a U2 piloted by Gary Powers in May 1960, the U2 was not immune to the threat from new ground-to-air missiles. British participation in U2 missions flown from British bases was discussed between Eisenhower and Macmillan at the same Bermuda conference at which the agreement to base Thor missiles in England was reached. These missions, flown under the closest veil of secrecy, included many dispatched from East Anglian bases, among them Lakenheath in Suffolk. Missions included ELINT (electronic intelligence) flights from RAF Watton in Norfolk, using Canberras fitted with sophisticated tape recorders to pick up Russian transmissions. Macmillan later admitted British participation in covert spy-flights when he wrote in his diaries that the British 'actually have flown some very successful ones [flights] with aeroplanes which the Americans gave us'.

The Soviet authorities were well aware that the UK was being used as a base for aerial espionage. On 1 July 1960 an American RB-47 aircraft equipped for detailed reconnaissance took off from Brize Norton in Oxfordshire. It never returned, having been tracked by Soviet fighters and shot down in Soviet territorial waters. The Kremlin sent a strong warning to the British Government, emphasising the dangerous consequences of allowing the American Air Force to mount 'provocative' missions from British territory. The

Americans denied that the aircraft was over Russian waters when it was chased and shot down, but the incident sparked a dispute in the British Parliament and raised questions as to whether the Attlee and Churchill agreements with President Truman covered covert spy-flights by the American Air Force from UK bases. Macmillan's answer was pretty unspecific: '... we have consultations and agreements for operations which we regard as essential, if there is to be a deterrent and if its value and strength is to be maintained.' Macmillan added, under further questioning, that there might be some who felt the presence of US bases in Britain constituted a threat to national security. But there were many more who felt that the absence of American bases here would be an even greater threat. Not surprisingly, he refused to be more explicit about the decision-making process before any operational use of nuclear forces stationed in the UK could be mounted, or before reconnaissance flights could be sanctioned, saying that to do so would not be in the national interest.

According to Thomas C. Reed, former Secretary of the US Air Force, writing in his book *At the Abyss*, it was the Canberra flight in August 1953 that rang the warning bells and prompted President Eisenhower to assemble a group of experts – the Teapot Committee – to plan a response and energise America's own rocket and missile programme, of which Thor was the first 'stop-gap' product. With a range of almost 2,000 miles, it made Great Britain, from the American point of view, the perfect launch pad. It gave the United States breathing space to complete the development of its own intercontinental ballistic missiles, while providing them with the counter to Soviet rockets capable of intercontinental warfare.

Although Churchill and Macmillan both sanctioned spy-flights from the UK, another British Prime Minister took a different line. During the summer of 1955 American U-2s were flown in to Lakenheath, together with pilots working nominally for the CIA. When the then Prime Minister, Anthony Eden, heard of the intention to mount a series of surveillance missions, he refused permission. This was shortly after the celebrated case of the British frogman, Commander Lionel Crabb, who went missing on a covert espionage exercise to learn the secrets of a Russian warship on a goodwill mission to the UK. This episode resulted in huge embarrassment for the British Government, and Eden in particular. The Americans transferred their U2s to Germany, where they flew missions from Wiesbaden with the approval of the West Germans.

Clearly, the West was not alone in seeking vital information on weapons capability. The Soviet Union had its own means of gaining intelligence about what was going on in East Anglia and in the rest of the UK on bases operated by the RAF and the American Strategic Air Command. Covert over-flights were not as practical over the UK as they were over the vast spaces of the USSR and its Warsaw Pact neighbours. But Russian intruder aircraft, routinely tracked by RAF fighters, flew close to the east coast several times a week throughout most of the Cold War period. Russian sources were capable of gleaning detailed information in other ways, as is clear from the extremely accurate KGB Soviet Cold War maps of East Anglia and its many operational bases now on display at the Air Defence Museum at Neatishead in Norfolk. They were produced by the Russian military between 1950 and the late 1980s, using aerial photographs, satellite images, and knowledge gleaned by KGB agents. Together the Russian maps covered over 6,000 square miles of the UK in the utmost detail, and included military and operational bases excluded from British Ordinance Survey maps. The Russian maps reveal the exact location and purpose of every structure of possible military importance. Even road widths, the heights of bridges and depth of rivers are detailed, together with bus and railway stations. Undoubtedly, the Soviet Union had all the important RAF and military sites in East Anglia pinpointed and targeted.

They knew that had they used their capability against American cities and bomber bases on American soil, the first Western response, in the period 1959–63, would have been launched from the East of England: that is, if USSR missiles had not eliminated the Thor bases first.

The Soviets knew where the Thor bases were. A scheduled Moscow–London civilian passenger service was conveniently in-augurated in 1958, using a Tupolev TU 104 jet airliner. The routine flights regularly seemed to suffer 'navigation errors' over the North Sea. This meant the aircraft often took a route which passed over one or more of the missile bases. The TU 104 had, for no clear commercial reason, a glazed nose providing an ideal observation position from which to photograph what was happening on the ground. British authorities knew that on occasions these over flights by Soviet bloc airliners involved dropping to lower altitudes and the crew temporarily switching off their onboard transponders which broadcast their position to air traffic controllers.

Some Cold War commentators think that the establishment of Thor as an operational force in the UK by May 1960 helped to restrain Khrushchev's potential response, in the aftermath of the shooting down over the Soviet Union of America's U2 spy-plane, and the capture of its pilot, Gary Powers. Khrushchev was in Paris for abortive summit talks when the U2 was downed. He issued an angry ultimatum that amounted to a demand to the USA to apologise 'or else'! The 'or else' he fleshed out in a further belligerent statement, threatening that if any aircraft violated Soviet frontiers again orders to shoot it down and bomb the base it had come from would be strictly carried out. The threat was sobering in the climate of the time. America refused to apologise, and the Soviet threat of possible armed consequences never materialised. Eyeball-to-eyeball confrontation during the Cuban crisis was still in the future. Was it the potential of the new force of sixty missiles aimed at the Soviet Union from Eastern England that helped to keep the peace during the tense facedown following the shooting down of America's spy-plane and the very public trial in Moscow of its pilot? Some commentators in the USA at the time wanted to believe that it was.

CHAPTER 7

Project Emily

In January 1957, soon after Duncan Sandys had been appointed Minister of Defence, he visited Washington for discussions with his American counterparts in the Pentagon. Following these meetings he sent Macmillan a telegram which clearly demonstrated how determined the Americans were to deploy ballistic missiles in England. He wrote,

> They are most anxious, in view of progress of the Russian ballistic rockets, that a rocket deterrent should be established in Britain as soon as possible. The United States would provide weapons and specialised equipment, including anything costing dollars. Nuclear warheads would be held under the same conditions as American nuclear bombs for British bombers. We would undertake site works and provide general supporting equipment. The United States estimate of the cost to us for the four sites is £10 million, apart from costs of personnel and their training and housing.

Sandys' telegram continued: 'The proposal would give us a megaton-rocket deterrent in Britain at least five years before we could provide it ourselves.'

Britain had commenced work on developing its own Blue Streak ballistic rocket, and in 1957 began building a rocket-testing ground at Spadeadam in Cumbria, but the British missile was a long way from becoming a reality. Ironically, at the time the Minister of

Defence was communicating with Macmillan, Thor was also an unproved weapon. But that was not allowed to stand in the way. The Soviet progress in rocket science dictated there had to be confidence that Thor would prove successful. The Americans put formal proposals to the UK on 1 February. In doing so they suggested that in view of the importance of deploying a ballistic deterrent at the earliest possible date on British soil, a 'crash programme' should be put in hand. This, they told the British, could provide an experimental squadron of five missiles, deployed at a USAF base in the UK by July 1958, operated and paid for by the USA. Meanwhile, work would commence on four regular sites to be operated by the RAF. As soon as the RAF sites were operational the USAF experimental unit would be disbanded.

By June service-to-service discussions were taking place between the USAF and the RAF. One issue raised was the potential danger to the British civilian population if the Americans were to site missiles on one of their UK Strategic Air Force bases in the centre of the country – Brize Norton had been mooted – which would have meant using a trajectory passing either over the London area or over the city of Oxford. The British, mindful of the dangers and the appalling consequences of a mis-launch or accidental explosion, suggested using sites on the east coast, which had been earmarked for Blue Streak. Arguments were raised over British concerns at the vulnerability of Thor. It had not been designed to be fired from a hardened underground silo, as Blue Streak was planned to be. In fact little thought had been given to protecting Thor from a Soviet pre-emptive strike. Initial discussions showed that the USAF, to achieve rapid operational capability, was planning to locate the first thirty missiles on just two sites, increasing their vulnerability from a well-aimed Russian missile still further. One incoming Soviet missile could have destroyed all thirty Thors in a single blow.

Joint discussions at ministerial level, and between senior officers from the RAF and USAF, continued throughout the summer and autumn of 1957, as development testing of Thor proceeded in the United States. Meanwhile, building of the American alternative IRBM, the Jupiter rocket, progressed in tandem with Thor. It was not until December that the British Chiefs of Staff were informed definitively by their American colleagues that it was Thor and not Jupiter that would be deployed in England.

By January 1958 a draft technical agreement had been hammered out, naming four main missile squadron bases. A first concept, under which two units would have been manned by the USAF and the other two by the RAF, gave way under pressure from the British government, to all four units being operated by the RAF. The Government was keen, despite the nuances of the inter-governmental agreement, to demonstrate publicly that the missiles would be part of Bomber Command, and under immediate British control. At this stage the dual-key launch procedure for Thor, requiring both an RAF officer and an American officer to activate separate stages of the launch, had not become a public issue. It would prove an on-going matter of comment and controversy as time went on.

It was at this stage that the Chief of Air Staff wrote a note expressing concern at the 'unsatisfactory state of affairs regarding the establishment of American IRBMs in the country', and put it before his colleague Chiefs of Staff. The note, forwarded to Ministers, made clear that the service chiefs were opposed to being railroaded into a commitment they considered was designed to serve American ends more than British. It was their view that this move was first and foremost an insurance policy for America. Whether it gave Britain any extra protection, or conversely exposed Britain to greater danger, was a matter of debate. The memorandum said that 'these highly vulnerable missiles' would make the UK a more attractive target. It raised new fears that there was a possibility the missiles based in the UK would ultimately come under the operational control of the Supreme Allied Commander Europe and the Commander-in-Chief US Air Forces in Europe, which could be detrimental to British interests. Such a situation could have inhibited the British Government from using Thor independently to defend UK national interests in a scenario where, for their own reasons, America or NATO held back. A further issue, as far as the Chiefs of Staff were concerned, was that if the project succeeded there would be pressure for Britain to abandon her own independent IRBM deterrent, Blue Streak. The latter point was pertinent – soon Blue Streak was abandoned.

Ministers took a different view. They were well aware of the disadvantages the service chiefs were voicing, but they insisted that the Chiefs of Staff should not take the negative line. The Cabinet debated the missile deployment on 12 February 1958, and authorised continued detailed negotiations with the US authorities. With an eye to possible public concerns, Government officials noted that land clearance and site works could raise delicate issues of public relations, and they advised a close watch on all activities which might come to public notice. Project Emily, despite having a name carefully chosen to allay fears, was beginning to alarm sections of the population. The concerns of officials at the Ministry of Defence were well founded, given the demonstrations mounted by the fledgling Campaign for Nuclear Disarmament that were to follow, when the public could see construction taking place at the launch sites.

Cabinet approved the draft agreement with the US Government on 18 February. On 25 February the proposed deployment became public knowledge with the publication of a White Paper entitled, 'Supply of Ballistic Missiles by the United States to the United Kingdom'. It said the missiles would be manned and operated by UK personnel who would be trained in the USA at the earliest feasible date. On the control of the missiles, the White Paper said a decision to launch would be a joint one between the two governments, but the warheads would remain in full US custody, as required by American law.

In a Parliamentary statement Duncan Sandys told the Commons: 'The nuclear warheads will remain in American custody and will be kept in an unarmed condition so that there can be no risk of a nuclear explosion; and the weapon is designed in such a way that it would be impossible for it to be launched accidentally.' He added that they would not be launched except 'by a joint positive decision' of both the British and United States governments. There would be special arrangements for ensuring rapid consultation, and the decision would be taken by both governments, and not, he emphasised, by military commanders.

Two days later up popped a senior American Air Force officer, a Colonel Zinc of the 705th Strategic Missile Wing in Britain, who to the consternation of both British and American governments claimed to have 'full operational control of the rockets and rocket bases in Britain'. His statement directly contradicted the agreement between the two governments, and in particular the assurances Duncan Sandys had given in Parliament, that the two governments and not the military would decide if and when the missiles were to be used. Macmillan in his diary noted,

> There was a great flap this morning over an extraordinary statement by a Colonel Zinc – an American Eagle Colonel of the Air Force who claims to be about to take over command of the rockets/rocket bases in Britain. As this was in direct contradiction (a) to the terms of the agreement published last Monday and (b) what we told Parliament on Monday and in the debate yesterday, Colonel Zinc has put his foot in it on a grand scale.

Colonel Zinc was quickly put in his place by a statement from the Pentagon making it clear that he was only responsible for training RAF crews, but Macmillan sought clarification direct from the President, and Eisenhower reaffirmed the agreements made at the Bermuda conference. It was a minor hiccup, but the consequences reverberated around Westminster and clearly showed the sensitivities of the situation as far as the UK was concerned.

In practical terms concerns over command and control of the Thor missiles were real. The complexity of the international chain of command involved in authenticating the dual-key release of the nuclear-armed missiles was horrifying. On the American side it involved an order that started with the President and involved Strategic Air Command in the States, 7th Air Division in the UK and the US Air Force units who controlled the nuclear warheads at each Thor squadron base. On the British side a simultaneous order needed to originate from the Prime Minister and travel through Bomber Command Headquarters via Group headquarters to the launch officers at the individual missile squadrons.

Subsequently, RAF launch crews might have disputed the Sandys point in relation to dual-key control. The technology, particularly early on, was certainly capable of being manipulated. The dual-key system, under which officers of each nation had to insert separate keys to ensure a launch, was by no means foolproof technology, and it could be overridden. A letter to *The Times* in

September 1974 written by Donald Hofford, a retired RAF officer, cast light on this. He recalled that he was observing a simulated launch of a Thor missile, and as the point in the launch process came when the American authentication officer was required to use his war/peace key to arm the warhead, the officer had failed to arrive. The situation was saved by an RAF launch officer's 'adroit use of a screwdriver in the keyhole' to enable the simulated

The twenty Thor IRBM launch sites in Yorkshire and East Anglia, 1959–63.

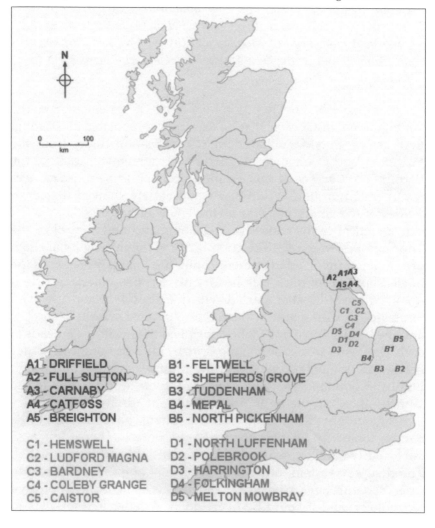

A1 - DRIFFIELD
A2 - FULL SUTTON
A3 - CARNABY
A4 - CATFOSS
A5 - BREIGHTON

B1 - FELTWELL
B2 - SHEPHERD'S GROVE
B3 - TUDDENHAM
B4 - MEPAL
B5 - NORTH PICKENHAM

C1 - HEMSWELL
C2 - LUDFORD MAGNA
C3 - BARDNEY
C4 - COLEBY GRANGE
C5 - CAISTOR

D1 - NORTH LUFFENHAM
D2 - POLEBROOK
D3 - HARRINGTON
D4 - FOLKINGHAM
D5 - MELTON MOWBRAY

launch to continue. There were many other such stories circulating among the British crews.

Alarm bells rang in communities down England's east coast when Duncan Sandys told MPs that the missiles would be deployed in small numbers on dispersed sites, mostly on active or disused RAF airfields, mainly in East Anglia, Lincolnshire and Yorkshire. He told the Commons that sites for the rocket bases would be kept secret. But residents in quiet country villages and market towns quickly realised that nuclear-tipped rockets were to be stationed at launch pads in their neighbourhoods. There was no disguising the elaborate site works required. The reality that the Cold War was coming close to rural doorsteps in a frightening new guise came first in Norfolk, when a minute was circulated confirming that the first RAF Thor complex would have its main base at Feltwell, near Thetford. Three launch pads were to be built on the former war-time airfield, and associated with it would be four other satellite launch sites, each housing three missiles, at North Pickenham in Norfolk, Shepherd's Grove and Tuddenham in Suffolk, and Mepal in Cambridgeshire.

Unknown by the public certain safety parameters were laid down against which the sites were assessed. They included a less than reassuring rule that no missile was to be sited within 1,500 feet of an inhabited building or within 750 feet of a public road.

This announcement was followed a few weeks later with the news that Hemswell in Lincolnshire would be the main base for the second Thor complex. Its satellite launch pads were to be at Bardney, Caistor, Ludford Magna and Coleby Grange.

Despite progress on the ground, and political resolution to see ballistic missiles on British bases, there was still real concern being expressed in the higher echelons of the RAF about Thor's operational readiness. The Chief of the Air Staff, Air Chief Marshal Sir Dermot Boyle, voiced the view that it would be wrong to deploy Thor as an operational weapon until the Chiefs of Staff collectively were satisfied the missile could function safely and efficiently. He was worried, he said, at pressure from the Americans to deploy Thor before 'we can be satisfied that it has achieved a satisfactory operational performance'. Undoubtedly Sir Dermot was as apprehensive about launch safety, and the possible catastrophic consequences for the civilian population of an accident, as he was on obtaining evidence that Thor was accurate and effective as a weapon. These concerns rumbled on. They even triggered some adverse reports in the British press. But political will and American determination to have the means to confront Russia's potential lead in the missile stakes overcame the doubts from the top of the British military. Meanwhile, the news from across the Atlantic was improving. As the Thor test programme continued, confidence grew in the missile's capability, although it was clear that until RAF crews had been trained and had actually undertaken a successful launch themselves, RAF scepticism would remain.

Even when, in September 1958, the first UK missile squadron, based at Feltwell, had been authorised, doubts were being expressed about the formation of more than one further squadron. The Secretary of State for Air, in a memorandum to the Minister of Defence in early 1959, said that operationally there were no grounds to justify 'taking weapons for the second squadron', since Thor was still under development, and no single missile had as yet attempted a full operational test, or been tried out over the full 1,500-nautical-mile range. He recommended no commitment to a third and fourth squadron 'until we are satisfied that the weapon development programme is proceeding satisfactorily'.

Ministers and senior officers remained sensitive to the public and political issues of Thor's forthcoming arrival in the UK. So sensitive, indeed, that for the American teams involved in site selection there was a real 'cloak-and-dagger' feel. American officers were told to dress in civilian clothes. It was understood that any talking would be done by British personnel to ensure American accents were not identified. Only RAF vehicles were used for travel, and elaborate cover stories were employed to avoid open discussion of guided-missile sites. Negotiations about construction were explained away as providing aircraft parking bays rather than missile-launch emplacements. As things progressed, the Government was worried that the public would misinterpret the arrival of hundreds of American civilian engineers and technicians, and assume a USAF take-over. A paper sent to the Secretary of State for Air warned that the prospect of some forty American civilians from the Douglas Aircraft Company arriving at Feltwell, to be accommodated in a small caravan 'town', would inevitably lead to comment and rumour. Their numbers would swell progressively until about 400 were accommodated at the base, working on installing the technical infrastructure. Such large numbers of American civilians would inevitably create a major talking-point in the villages surrounding the site.

There were similar concerns in other parts of the country. RAF personnel reporting for duty at RAF Driffield were surprised to find signs to 'Santa Monica-on-the-Wolds', the name the Douglas employees conjured up for their trailer park there. The government memorandum also drew attention to the fact that the missiles destined for the RAF had United States Air Force emblems prominently painted on them, which 'could be quite embarrassing when they are noticed by the people of Feltwell and the surrounding villages'. Apart from anything else it would raise questions about where ultimate responsibility lay for this new generation of nuclear weapons, between the British and US authorities. The issue was sufficiently sensitive to lead to authorisation – subject to American agreement, it should be noted – to change the USAF markings to RAF roundels.

In Norfolk the local daily newspaper, *Eastern Daily Press*, came out with a headline on 10 September 1958 declaring 'Norfolk Rocket Base "Locals" May Not See Missile Yet'. In a news story I recall filing as a local journalist, I said that in spite of reports that the gigantic 65 ft Thor missile would be delivered to its launching site near Feltwell within the following few days, people living near Britain's first rocket base were sceptical. The local parish council had not received any official indication that a missile site was being developed within the parish boundaries, and they were concerned that a road would have to be closed as part of the development of the base. Householders who lived along the road were getting worried, as their windows now looked out onto a skyline of towers, concrete blast-walls and fuel tanks. My report went on: 'In May what was a grass field has grown rapidly into something resembling a small village. Long concrete roads and massive blast-walls have been constructed, and floodlights on tall standards sprout over a wide area. The whole base is surrounded by barbed-wire fences and a tall wire-mesh fence.'

Two days later the looming presence of Thor in the East Anglian countryside drew more headlines in the *EDP*:

While work went on with all possible speed yesterday on Britain's first rocket site near Feltwell, progress was reported on what is probably a second site near Walsham Le Willows, the quiet Suffolk village a few miles from the Norfolk border. With the calmness of a rural community that has long known and accepted the presence of American jet aircraft in the district, people in the north-east corner of West Suffolk appear to be getting used to the idea that they will soon have what they believe will be a rocket missile site in their midst. For some weeks contractors have been working on the site which is near Walsham Le Willows, a village nine miles from Diss. Anyone using a particular local road can see the large concrete structures that are being built. Notices give warning of guard dogs and the site is protected by barbed wire fences.

This in fact was to be the Shepherd's Grove launch site, part of the Feltwell complex. The paper reported that a local farmer summed up the reaction of villagers: 'I think we have to grin and bear it' appeared typical of the feeling in the district. 'No matter what we say it will make no difference.'

The first Thor site in the UK continued to attract local media attention. On 17 September the *EDP* carried a further report from my office on a 'dummy run' for the Thor transporter. 'Specially trained RAF men are being trained to carry the rocket safely from Lakenheath Airbase, where it was flown secretly recently, to the launching pad. Yesterday along the country road between the airbase and the missile base a crew were practising with the 90 ft transporter-launcher which will be used to carry the Thor.' The newspaper reported that the transporter was escorted by two RAF police outriders on motor-cycles and preceded by an RAF police vehicle. Following it was a staff car carrying the American officer in charge of the operation.

Three days later, on 20 September, as members of the local press, colleagues and I were actually invited to Feltwell to see Britain's first nuclear ballistic missile, which had been delivered early in the morning of the previous day. 'Thor Now In RAF Hands At No. 1 Base Near Feltwell', the headline announced. The report noted that the missile had been masked by a canvas cover during its trip through the Norfolk countryside. Once at Feltwell, the cover was removed, revealing the RAF colours and the number '01' painted on the rocket. The report further pointed out that photographers were kept back twenty-five yards from the missile. It continued: 'The programme now follows two parallel courses – the build-up of missile experience in the RAF squadrons in Britain, and the continuation of tests in the United States.'

I well recall that the authorities were clearly at pains to point out to the local press, and through the press to the local population, that there was minimum risk of accident. 'A number of safety devices remove risk', my report stated. 'In the event of any failure over friendly territory the Thor can be destroyed harmlessly.' That may have been a comfort to people living under the missile's flight path, but it was an assertion former launch crew members would deny. Any means of communicating a destruct signal to the rocket would have enabled an enemy to do the same, and so negate the weapon's purpose, though it was true that the final arming of the nuclear warhead did not take place until the last stage of the missile's trajectory towards its target.

Perhaps it was a more trusting world and people had become used to living daily under the Cold War threat. But it is interesting to note that on the same day as the first Thor arrived at the first British launch site, in Norfolk alone over 7,000 men and women had been enrolled and trained as volunteers in Civil Defence detachments. Nationally, Civil Defence numbered some 500,000.

It was not long before nuclear war protestors from the fledgling Campaign For Nuclear Disarmament, or as it was called then, the Direct Action Committee Against Nuclear War, began to take notice of what was happening in the British countryside.

On 6 December 1958, *Eastern Daily Press* reporters, myself among them, witnessed the beginnings of anti-nuclear protest that would become familiar as the Cold War years progressed. The opening salvoes were dramatic and surprisingly violent, as the headlines in the local Norfolk press recorded: 'Hot Reception for Protest Marchers at Thor Base' … 'Demonstrators in Mud Melée' … 'Norfolk Organiser talks of "Appalling rough Treatment".' Nearly fifty demonstrators actually gained entry to the base at North

Pickenham, near Swaffham, bridging barbed-wire entanglements by placing placards over the sharp wire barbs and scrambling across. Many clambered onto the massive concrete mixing plant in the centre of the base, as I and other reporters witnessed, stopping work from proceeding. 'Yelling abuse, the construction workers grabbed men and women alike,' the *EDP* report recorded, 'and hurled them into a six-inch-deep mixture of mud and wet concrete. Women were dragged along by their hair and many were trampled on while trying to release themselves in the sea of mud.' The report went on to say that several demonstrators were treated for minor injuries, and two who got wet concrete into their eyes were taken to hospital at King's Lynn and detained for treatment. 'RAF firemen turned their hoses on the intruders, but they ran through streaming jets of water into the centre of the site', the report continued. 'Demonstrators were pushed, kicked, trapped and punched as the situation reached a near riot. Many were in a pitiful condition, soaked by hoses, covered head to foot in mud and with rapidly drying concrete matted in their hair.' One worker, after seeing what had gone on, was reported as saying, 'I am ashamed to be working on this site.'

The *EDP* was robust in its condemnation of the handling of the protest by the authorities. In a leader it confessed to being 'shocked and perplexed by the way in which the demonstration was handled or mishandled by the authorities. It looks as if the workers were left to do something the authorities did not care to do for themselves – and the law connived at its own contempt. If there had been Russian spies concealed in a nearby ditch they must have ached with laughter. For to combat passive resistance by condoning private violence is not a shining example of democratic or indeed any other form of government. It is simply an abdication of responsibility.'

The following day, a Sunday, twenty demonstrators again managed to enter the North Pickenham site. This time the contractors, many of whom were Irish migrant workers without any affiliation to trade unions, took no action and left it to the RAF security police to remove the protestors.

What happened in Norfolk drew considerable national media attention, and on 9 December the Air Minister, George Ward, was closely questioned in Parliament over the events at the North Pickenham Thor base. He told MPs he did not think any more force than was necessary was used, and the Government would consider what steps might be necessary to prevent recurrences of the scenes that had taken place over the previous weekend. The local MP for South-West Norfolk, Labour member Sidney Dye, told the House he had been there to witness what had happened. Work had been hampered for several hours on each day. He asked why more robust security fencing was not erected while site works continued.

Another Labour member, Mr R.T. Paget from Northampton, voicing the Opposition's concerns that Thor was essentially a first-strike weapon, asked, 'What in the world is the use of a deterrent which can be knocked out before it can possibly be launched, unless we propose to be the aggressor?'

Another Labour MP, Mr G.R. Chetwynd, representing Stockton, questioned the continuing secrecy surrounding the locations of the Thor launch sites. Referring to the Direct Action Committee Against Nuclear War, he queried why this organisation knew the addresses of the launch pads. Wasn't it time the House of Commons was also told? In reply the Minister said, to Labour jeers, 'There is a very great difference between a forced entry on one or two sites by these demonstrators and official confirmation by the Air Ministry.' And, he added, the Thor launch emplacements were a valuable part of the Western deterrent, and the Government would certainly continue to build sites undeterred by any demonstrations.

Locally, it seems, the population were more resigned to the new nuclear-armed missiles in their midst. A letter writer to the editor of the EDP was indignant, though not about the missiles themselves, or about the violent protests they attracted, but about the fact that the BBC, in its national coverage, had described Swaffham as a village, and not a market town!

Undeterred by what had taken place over the weekend of 6/7 December, the demonstrators came back for more three days before Christmas. I witnessed a ninety-strong contingent of demonstrators who marched from Swaffham the few miles to the village of North Pickenham. Forty-five demonstrators were arrested by Norfolk police. Twenty-two refused to give an undertaking not to take part in further demonstrations, and they were held in custody over the Christmas holidays. Miss Pat Arrowsmith, one of the main organisers of the protest, was reported as saying, 'We want to try to get the unions to make it a "black" site so that no union members will work there.' The demonstrators, not many of whom were local, were not universally welcomed. When they formed up in Swaffham market-place for the march on the base, some stallholders pelted them with rotten fruit. Others attempted to drown out speakers at the rally by revving their car engines. At North Pickenham base many of the civilian workmen, whose massive concrete mixers the protestors again tried to commandeer and prevent from operating, jeered them.

News of the campaign to disrupt work on the sites spread fast and far. The day after the demonstration at North Pickenham, the Clerk to Swaffham District Council, James Dunn, received a phone call from a journalist in Moscow. The Russian newsman said he had read reports of the Swaffham protest and asked how many had taken part, and about the role of the police. To Mr Dunn's surprise he also enquired how many had been taken to hospital and the extent of their injuries. Having stressed that the demonstration had on this occasion been peaceful, and that no one had been hurt, Mr Dunn ended the conversation by wishing everyone in Moscow a 'Happy Christmas!'

When those who had been held in custody appeared at Swaffham Magistrates Court, after the Christmas holidays, they were represented at the hearing, which lasted over seven hours, by two London barristers. Col. J.H. Boag, chairman of the magistrates, told the demonstrators,

> Nobody wants to make martyrs of you. We are here to uphold the civil law. People in this country are allowed to express, and with a great deal of publicity, views which are often contrary to the government of the day. That right is upheld by law. You have been tried, not for your views, but because you challenged the law, which in the last resort will uphold your freedom of expression.

Norman Oster, one of the London barristers defending the protestors, told the court, 'They believe it quite wrong to build and create rocket bases and manufacture nuclear weapons. And they believe if this continues a nuclear war, which could destroy the human race, will result. In international law this would amount to genocide.'

The other barrister, Mr Greville Janner, said, 'No case quite like this has occurred before, certainly not since the days of the suffragettes. I beg you not to make martyrs of them in any way.' Most of those arrested were bound over to be of good behaviour for a year, with an alternative of fourteen days in prison. Some chose prison. The whole episode drew considerable national coverage. The Campaign for Nuclear Disarmament was in its early stages, and Britain had not seen many similar demonstrations where determined, but largely peaceful, direct action, had been used on such a scale.

Through the closing months of 1958 and the spring of 1959, technical equipment and missiles were being flown into American and British bases in the UK in a steady stream. Both the first two squadrons had received their full complement by the end of April 1959. As more encouraging news of Thor test firings emerged in the USA, there was agreement that there could be no further cause to delay receipt of missiles for the third and fourth squadrons. These two launch complexes would be based at Driffield in East Yorkshire, with dispersed launch sites at Catfoss, Full Sutton, Carnaby and Breighton, and North Luffenham in the East Midlands, with satellite bases at Polebrook, Harrington (both in Northamptonshire), Melton Mowbray (Leicestershire) and Folkingham (Lincolnshire).

Thor's operational capability was finally acknowledged publicly on 9 December 1959. A statement in Parliament by the Secretary of State for Air, George Ward, who was replying to an MP's question, said, 'As a result of the test firings which have taken place in the USA, and in the light of the progress made in the training programme, we are now satisfied that Thor is able to take its place as part of the operational front line of the Royal Air Force.' With that statement, a unique, but brief, chapter in RAF history opened. The RAF was entering the rocket age.

On 16 December 1958 the first Thor launched by American service personnel of the 392nd Missile Training Squadron, under Strategic Air Command control, successfully lifted off its pad at Vandenberg. In an official comment the Americans stated that this successful launch should 'go far to offset the under-the-surface concern in the UK about the weapon'. It should inspire confidence that the date set for it to be brought into operational service in England could be met.

Work on preparing the UK sites had began in late 1957, with Feltwell as the lead location. Initial survey work was carried out at all the chosen locations by 13 Field Squadron of the Royal Engineers, based at Fernhurst Camp in Sussex. Extremely accurate astrogeodetic surveying of each one of the sixty launch pads was essential for the missile's guidance system to be configured to steer the warhead to its distant target. The guidance system needed to know precisely where its flight started in order to drop the warhead accurately on the target for which it was destined.

The twenty sites scattered down the East of England were located, within the four Thor complexes, a minimum of ten and a maximum of thirty miles apart. This wide geographical spread was insisted upon so that an incoming Soviet warhead aimed at one site could not destroy other launch pads in the same complex. The fixed elements of the installations – concrete launch pads, revetment blast-walls, underground conduits, security fences and lighting pillars, were constructed by British contractors. The ground works were extensive, requiring excavation of 600,000 cu yd of earth, filling in a further 400,000 cu yd, and pouring 235,000 cu yd of concrete, plus driving in nearly 500 deep piles to prevent settlement and ensure the foundations remained true to the geodetic survey. Each launch pad needed many tons of concrete, but even so the pads were only strong enough to withstand a single launch. Had the deterrent been fired, the inevitable counter-strike by the USSR would have been so destructive that it was considered there would never be a requirement for any launch pad to be used more than once.

The ground support equipment for each launch site added up to nearly two hundred major items. These were sub-contracted by Douglas to manufacturers across the United States. The units then had to be transported across the Atlantic to the remote sites down the East of England and fitted together to tight weapons-system specifications. These were complex units. They were assembled at sites in England even before they had been operationally tested in the United States, or a single missile launched using them. In truth, the whole complicated jigsaw had to work, and work first time. Amazingly, because of the breadth of detailed forward planning, it did work, and with very few major difficulties.

One of the basic problems Project Emily faced was how to house the hundreds of American technicians, servicemen and their families needed to install and equip the launch sites. This workforce was under pressure and time constraints, in unfamiliar surroundings, in remote and isolated locations. Douglas sent a senior employee, Bill Duval, over to England in December 1958 to take charge of the technical installation programme. His instructions were to keep the project on track and on time. As UK operations manager, his was an intensive, high-pressured, trouble-shooting role. Solving problems ranging from technical blips to personnel issues, it was a round-the-clock responsibility. As housing was at a premium, leases were taken on several country mansions in East Anglia, including Lynford Hall near Thetford, and Brandon Park. This, however, was only a partial solution. The Douglas work-force was expanding fast, from several hundred to close to a thousand. The answer, Duval decided, was to provide trailer parks. The Americans engaged British caravan companies to build residential trailers to American specifications, fitted with everything from washing machines to refrigerators. In the late 1950s caravans to such a high specification were unheard-of by British standards. The Americans missed their Officers' Clubs and their Air Force Exchange Facilities, and so the Douglas Company, aware of the need to maintain morale, set up and equipped social clubs, colloquially called Emily Clubs, at the four headquarters' construction sites, providing American-style juke-boxes and cinemas. Trailer-based medical centres were brought in with nursing staff flown over from California. It all helped to maintain momentum and morale through the cold, foggy winter of 1958/9.

An aircraft hangar at each of the four headquarters sites was modified to provide the administrative, technical and operational control for each Thor complex. These were referred to as the RIM building, RIM standing for Reception, Inspection and Maintenance. It was the missile man's equivalent of a second-line servicing hangar for aircraft, and it was where servicing and routine inspection of missiles was to take place. Special maintenance bays with false ceilings and air conditioning were provided, in which the more sensitive components like the propulsion, guidance, electronics and hydraulics systems were worked on, and in which detailed calibration could be undertaken. A brick extension to the RIM building contained the Missile Control Centre for each complex of fifteen launch pads. Manned twenty-four hours a day, every day of the year, these would be the nerve centres of the Thor force, in continuous contact with headquarters of Bomber Command, and via Bomber Command with the headquarters of Strategic Air Command in the United States.

Separate from the RAF buildings at each headquarters site, fenced-off storage enclosures for the nuclear warheads were con-structed. This was exclusively the American zone of responsibility. Guarded by armed USAF personnel, it was here that the warheads and their re-entry vehicles were to be stored, inspected and main-tained. Also in this secure compound the Americans received and initiated warhead-release procedures. Surrounded by high security, these buildings were virtually a no-go area for British service personnel, whatever their seniority. Few RAF personnel ever entered the nuclear storage area, and this extended even to the group captain in overall command of each Thor complex. The Americans jealously guarded their absolute control of the nuclear element of Thor.

Similar classified nuclear storage buildings and enclosures were provided at the satellite launch bases. Each had a one-bay storage building guarded by armed USAF personnel and a pyrotechnic store. The Americans operated a two-man policy to ensure that no one would ever be left alone near a nuclear warhead. The pyro-technic stores held the rocket igniters.

Each launch base, at the main complex and at the satellite locations, had three launch pads. Some 700 feet distant from the nearest pad was the designated launch-control area. This accom-modated the control trailer with its launch-control console, a checkout trailer, four mobile generators and a 5,000 gal oil tank for fuel for the diesel generators. Each of the three launch pads was equipped with a retractable shelter or missile hangar running on rails to protect the missile in its prone position on its erector-

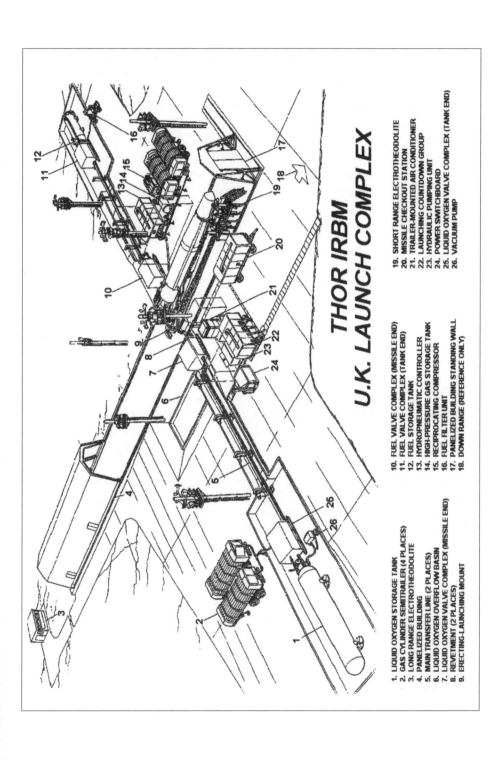

THOR IRBM
U.K. LAUNCH COMPLEX

1. LIQUID OXYGEN STORAGE TANK
2. GAS CYLINDER SEMITRAILER (4 PLACES)
3. LONG RANGE ELECTROTHEODOLITE
4. PANELIZED BUILDING
5. MAIN TRANSFER LINE (2 PLACES)
6. LIQUID OXYGEN OVERFLOW BASIN
7. LIQUID OXYGEN VALVE COMPLEX (MISSILE END)
8. REVETMENT (2 PLACES)
9. ERECTING-LAUNCHING MOUNT

10. FUEL VALVE COMPLEX (MISSILE END)
11. FUEL VALVE COMPLEX (TANK END)
12. FUEL STORAGE TANK
13. HYDROPNEUMATIC CONTROLLER
14. HIGH-PRESSURE GAS STORAGE TANK
15. RECIPROCATING COMPRESSOR
16. FUEL FILTER UNIT
17. PANELIZED BUILDING STANDING WALL
18. DOWN RANGE (REFERENCE ONLY)

19. SHORT RANGE ELECTROTHEODOLITE
20. MISSILE CHECKOUT STATION
21. TRAILER-MOUNTED AIR CONDITIONER
22. LAUNCHING COUNTDOWN GROUP
23. HYDRAULIC PUMPING UNIT
24. POWER SWITCHBOARD
25. LIQUID OXYGEN VALVE COMPLEX (TANK END)
26. VACUUM PUMP

transporter. The liquid oxygen and RP-1 (kerosene) that fuelled the missile were stored apart from each other at either side of the emplacement, a necessary precaution to guard against the possibility of spontaneous combustion. Stainless-steel piping was used to feed the super-cooled LOX, which had a boiling point of -183 °C, to the missile. A LOX dump tank was also provided in case the oxidiser needed to be rapidly discharged. Support trailers and other essential equipment were located behind L-shaped blast-walls. Thor was a one-shot weapon installed in England as quickly and as cheaply as possible. If ever fired, it was recognised the pad would have been unable to be used again. Even though the launch-control trailer was located at what was regarded as a safe distance from the nearest launch pad, the crew inside would have been subjected to deafening noise and an unnerving battering from the immense blast had one missile been launched, never mind three in quick succession. Some estimated the ground would shake up to several miles away. The local population would have been left in no doubt what had happened, and nothing was more certain than that within minutes an incoming missile would be targeting them.

The build-up of Thor in the UK was made possible by a massive American airlift, flying missiles and associated equipment to airheads at Lakenheath for Feltwell, Scampton for Hemswell, Leconfield for Driffield and Cottesmore for North Luffenham. A total airlift of more than 11.3 million kilograms of missiles and ground support equipment was flown in by American transport aircraft, operated by the 1607th Air Transport Wing. Nearly 6,000 tons of missiles and equipment was delivered to Feltwell alone, entailing some 300 flights from California by way of Newfoundland and the Azores.

Long Beach Municipal Airport in California, which was adjacent to the Douglas plant, was the main transport point for the airlift to Lakenheath. Air movements were so frequent that local residents at Long Beach protested at the increased traffic and noise.

At a local community meeting a leading American Air Force general appealed for understanding of the national importance to the United States of obtaining rapid operational readiness for the Thor bases in England.

The nature of the cargo in the missile airlift demanded that pilots should adopt special flying techniques. The rate of descent, for instance, was restricted to prevent pressure damage to the missile's fuel tanks. When guidance units were on board, take-offs were subject to exacting limitations. The guidance-unit gyroscopes cost thousands of dollars each, and were suspended in a lubricant that had to be maintained within strict temperature ranges throughout the flight. The control of this depended upon a consistent level of power being supplied from the aircraft. To maintain the necessary level pilots had to keep their engines throttled up to 1,200 rpm, even while awaiting take-off clearance. That meant holding the aircraft on the brakes against the pull of the propellers. While airborne the gauges had to be constantly checked. The flights were accompanied by so-called 'birdwatchers', whose task was to watch the gauges for signs of trouble. On landing, a battery system cut in to keep the heat within tolerable range until ground power could take over. When the missiles were off-loaded problems still remained. Their considerable size – 65 ft long – posed real difficulties delivering them down narrow country roads and through towns and villages.

The first phase of Thor missiles airlifted to England did not have all the refinements that were built in to those delivered later in the programme. They were basically research and development models aimed at early operational readiness, illustrating the urgency which ran like a thread through the whole of the Thor development and deployment. Later these missiles were modified at their launch sites, so the whole RAF armoury of IRBMs kept pace with major changes made on the production lines.

The build-up was rapid. In February 1959 sixty-three aircraft delivered hundreds of tons of equipment to Hemswell in Lincolnshire via RAF Scampton, direct from Southern California. Seventy-six flights were made to Driffield in Yorkshire, via RAF Leconfield.

The pace of the programme was incessant, driven by continuing threats emerging from the Soviet Union. In January 1959 Khrushchev boasted that the USSR had ballistic missiles in 'serial production'. He hinted his factories were 'turning them out like sausages'. That was certainly an exaggeration, and this was later proved to be the case. But at the time the USA and the UK could not afford to question it. Meanwhile, the Americans were having their own successes. Through March, April, May and June 1959, repeated test firings produced amazing accuracy at long and short range. On 6 October, a flight distance of 1,800 miles was chalked up, putting another 300-mile segment of the Communist Bloc within range of the UK-based missiles.

By the time the huge air haul was over, and construction and installation completed, Project Emily was recognised as one of the most successful co-ordinated efforts ever achieved for any weapons system. Air Vice-Marshal Stuart Menaul, in his book *Countdown*, described it as

> *a lesson on how military objectives can be completed on time and according to plan when the will to meet contractual agreements is present and the urgency of the project demands and gets high priority ... By using existing individual systems and components of known and proven design to the maximum extent, the Thor weapons system was fully operational in the UK just four and a half years after signing the original design contract. By adhering to a policy of progressive development in the field, in which information was fed back to the design and development teams at the manufacturers, many improvements were incorporated in the missiles, resulting in superior performance and improved reliability. In the latter part of the life of Thor, for example, the countdown was reduced by nearly half.*

That was the military view. Some Opposition MPs in the House of Commons thought differently. In March 1960, the month the last of the missiles was delivered to the UK, Labour MP John Strachey told the Government that Thor was 'terrifyingly vulnerable, highly immobile and menacing'. He described its deployment as one of the most reckless decisions ever taken by any British government.

CHAPTER 8

The Thor Squadrons

The arrival of Thor in the UK triggered the formation of more squadrons than at any other period of the RAF's peacetime history. More significantly, the establishment of twenty Thor squadrons meant that Bomber Command grew by the equivalent of sixty additional V-bombers, or the destructive power of an extra seven-and-a-half V-force squadrons. Each Thor IRBM, like a single Victor, Valiant or Vulcan aircraft of the V-force, could deliver a megaton-range warhead.

Initially, it was intended that each Thor complex, of headquarters site and four satellite launch bases, would constitute a single squadron, the associated launch sites in each complex being given Flight status. Thus Feltwell and its satellites became No. 77 (SM) Squadron, Hemswell in Lincolnshire 97 (SM) Squadron, North Luffenham in Leicestershire No. 144 (SM) Squadron, and Driffield in Yorkshire No. 98 (SM) Squadron. But the structure of the Thor force was soon revised. Each separate launch site, equipped with three missiles, was allocated a squadron denomination. Each squadron consisted of five flights. One flight was always on duty and at immediate readiness throughout its eight hour shift. Each flight was commanded by a flight lieutenant, the launch control officer, who was assisted by a master aircrew in the launch control trailer and one missile maintenance technician, or MMT, on each pad. There was also a missile systems analysis technician, or

69

MSAT, who worked for the squadron as a whole. Attached to each RAF squadron was a small group of USAF officers who were totally responsible for the nuclear warheads, their maintenance and arming. The headquarters units, together with their associated squadrons, comprised a Thor Wing. Individual squadron commanders were responsible to the Wing Commander Operations. The Wing Commander 'Ops' had four operations officers – later to be retitled missile controllers – working to him in the control centre of the RIM building. The missile control centre was permanently manned by an RAF squadron leader, who was missile controller for the entire wing. A USAF authentication controller, of lieutenant-colonel or major rank, sat alongside him. The operations room displayed the readiness state of all sixty missiles in Bomber Command, not just those within the complex. This enabled any of the four headquarters bases to assume launch control of the whole missile force, should Bomber Command headquarters ever be put out of action.

A wing commander (technical) was responsible for the technical personnel appointed to each squadron, and was in charge of the servicing of the missiles and launch equipment across all five sites. Maintenance was by progressive servicing, the objective being that each missile remained in an operational state most of the time. Every thirty days a periodic servicing team from the main base would visit a dispersed site, in which case it might be necessary for a missile to be out of commission for a few hours. This schedule was developed by the RAF from the original American service documents. But the RAF quickly wrote their own maintenance procedures, and some of the RAF technicians became much more knowledgeable about the servicing system than the USAF experts or even the Douglas engineers. They were frequently consulted by the Thor manufacturers about problems as they arose. Several modifications were introduced into the missile systems during their deployment in the UK, mainly to improve safety and to ease servicing rather than to improve performance. Although ballistic missiles were an entirely new departure for the RAF, the service rapidly implemented a command structure that closely matched the accepted hierarchy on more traditional flying stations. The staff allocated to a squadron of three missiles comprised five flights.

Each flight was under the control of a launch control officer, usually a flight lieutenant, and he was assisted by an assistant LCO, normally of master aircrew rank, plus three missile maintenance technicians (MMTs). In addition to the five flights, each squadron had its commanding officer, a squadron leader, plus a missile systems analyst, generally of chief technician rank, a corporal fireman, and two cooks. An RAF police flight of one sergeant and twelve corporals was responsible for squadron security. The USAF presence at each squadron consisted of a commanding officer, usually of the rank of captain, and five authentication officers, generally 1st or 2nd lieutenants.

At every launch site the launch-control officer (LCO) in charge of each shift held the key required to initiate a missile launch. Because of the dual-key protocol these RAF LCOs were shadowed at each launch site by the USAF authentication officers. They were members of the USAF 99th Support Squadron, the American unit designated to take custody and control of the nuclear warheads on British soil. These were the men who held the second key, known as the war/peace key, with which to arm the Thor's nuclear warhead. While Thor remained operational in the UK there was always an American officer on duty at each launch pad wearing the war/peace key on a chain around his neck. The RAF launch controller received his orders via the Air Ministry and Headquarters Bomber Command. The USAF authentication officers received theirs from Headquarters Strategic Air Command in Nebraska in the USA through Headquarters Seventh Air Division at South Ruislip. A complex communications system was installed which enabled a launch order to be sent directly from the Bomber Command Operations Centre direct to each missile squadron. To avoid disruption as a result of enemy action or breakdown, alternative routes of communication were put in which allowed command to be maintained if Headquarters Bomber Command was destroyed.

The RAF officer's key, on the decision of the Prime Minister, initiated the countdown for a combat launch. The USAF officer's key, on the decision of the US President, activated the nuclear warhead. Both were needed for the missile to be fired in anger. That was the theory of dual control. But it was by no means a sophisticated or foolproof system, and it was widely claimed that personnel found ways in which the dual-key concept could be outflanked. There are stories of screwdrivers being used to bypass the American key and establish a positive contact, or of pressure being exerted on the control console to activate the lock. There may well have been ways of overcoming the double-lock procedure, but how many of the stories which went the rounds were true is another matter. It is a fact, however, that an American Senator visiting a British launch site early on in the Thor deployment saw enough to persuade him to take the issue up with the authorities on his return to the States, and work was carried out on the console desks to make accidental or unauthorised action to outflank the key system, if not impossible, then far more difficult.

Peter Rogers, who rose to the rank of group captain, was LCO at Caistor in Lincolnshire in the early days of the Thor deployment. He recalls hearing the microswitch, normally activated by the American war/peace key, make contact as he bounced the end of a pencil on part of the console. Clearly, this was a defective switch, but the incident caused quite some concern, and the switch was rapidly replaced.

This was not sophisticated electronic technology of the kind used in modern weapons systems. Bill Young, who commanded 82 Squadron, based at Shepherd's Grove in Suffolk, recalls:

> The two key connections met at the back of the launch console. It was discovered that the rear cover of the console was undone by four simple finger-tight screws for maintenance purposes. Thus it would have been quite possible for either service (British or American) to make the vital links without a second key. From then on the four offending screws were tagged and sealed with wax. With a wry smile the senior technician informed the squadron commander, 'It doesn't matter, sir, our men on the pads can just as easily make the connection down there!'

Most, if not all, of the senior personnel, in particular the RAF launch-control officers, were ex-aircrew, in RAF terms general-duties, or GD, officers. All missile crews were made up of full-time servicemen. No national service conscripts served on the Thor bases. One squadron CO remembers that most officers appointed to command a Thor launch site were personally interviewed by Air

Marshal Sir Kenneth Cross before attending the missile school at
RAF Feltwell and taking up their commands.

Normally the LCO was responsible for checking the guidance
readings on his three missiles and ensuring the theodolites, used
to set the missiles' aim, were maintained and accurate.

Operational status of the missiles was the responsibility of RAF
senior NCO missile maintenance technicians, three per shift, one
for each missile. Back-up support came from the systems analyst
technician. Either a corporal electrical equipment technician, or a
civilian employed by the Air Ministry works department, maintained the diesel generators in case of a power failure from the
national grid. Each launch team that constituted a flight did four
day shifts, four evening shifts and four night shifts, followed by
four days off. After four complete cycles of shifts the crews had a
sixteen-day leave period.

Two Thor complexes were created in each of the two Bomber
Command groups – Hemswell and Driffield in No. 1 Group, and
Feltwell and North Luffenham in No. 3 Group.

Feltwell's operations record book chronicles the stages leading
up to its establishment as the first-ever ballistic missile site in the
UK. It records that construction of the three launch emplacements
commenced in June 1958. On their completion in August, the
Douglas Aircraft Company missile engineers and technicians of
associated companies began the installation of the ground support
and launch equipment. The first Thor missile arrived on site in
November, and RAF personnel received first demonstrations of
the missiles and the launch equipment from the American civilian
technicians in January 1959. The three launch sites were handed
over to the RAF in March 1959, and the following month RAF
launch-crew training commenced. The accolade for the first launch
site to get all its three Thors to operational readiness simultaneously went to North Pickenham in Norfolk, one of the satellite
sites in the Feltwell complex.

American author Julian Hartt, in his book *The Mighty Thor*,
writing shortly after Feltwell had been established as the first
operational base, waxed almost lyrical:

> *This is the Anglo-American planting of Thor missiles, rising celery-
> white from the billiard-table green and flatness of Feltwell ... As you*

drive through the countryside you find some Thors lying somnolent under their retractable metal sheds. Others stand erect on sturdy boles of their eight-foot-wide metal trunks, getting their regular 'exercise'. Resting or standing, all impress the observer with their silent aura of lightly leashed power, and the terrible potency of the incongruously small button-nosed packages at their tips, controlled by USAF officers at each site.

He continued, further to impress his American readers thousands of miles from rural East Anglia:

This potential is respected. As angry-horned bulls are carefully fenced, more to protect the rural populace than the bulls, the Thors are similarly corralled in their pastoral setting. Each launching complex is surrounded by man-high horizontal coils of barbed wire. Outside are patrols of RAF troops and war dogs trained to be vicious. And through the night, the scene is whitewashed by floodlights.

Further north in Lincolnshire, the Hemswell pads, missiles and equipment were handed over to the RAF on 20 July 1959. The last Thor missile – Number 60 – was received at RAF Folkingham, Lincolnshire, part of the North Luffenham complex, on 1 April 1960. The North Luffenham complex was officially handed over at a ceremonial parade on 5 May, marking the final incorporation into the RAF of all four missile complexes, all twenty strategic missile squadrons, and all sixty Thor rockets. At that point, the official conclusion of Project Emily, Thor constituted a deterrent force of far greater destructive potential than all the bombs of all the wars that had gone before.

The conclusion of Project Emily was marked by a parade at North Luffenham. Bill Duval, in a message to his army of Douglas technicians, said,

Emily has been a gal of many moods, delightful at times and perfectly horrid on other occasions. She was a thing of beauty, an ugly wench, a lovely lady, a nagging shrew, a light-hearted child, a serious, worrying mother ... She was to say the least an interesting female, and one we shall never forget. I am sad that the time has come to leave her ....

Bill Duval spoke as though Emily was a real live girl. In fact she was. The true story emerged fifty years later when in his retirement Rowland Hall, the Air Ministry Directorate of Works official, who created the mass of technical drawings required for the building of the sixty Thor launch pads in England, recalled how a pin-up model played a major role in Cold War history. Rowland told me: 'It is interesting how the project received its code name. I was given a Pirelli calendar with a scantily clad female on it and her name Emily in small print below.' The lady clearly made an impression on Hall. 'I decided to stencil her name in large letters and pin the picture on the office notice board.' The next door office in the Air Ministry was occupied by a small group of USAF representatives from the US 7th Air Division whose function was to administer the Thor project in the UK in its initial stages and to sanction the work the Air Ministry was undertaking in preparation for the massive civil engineering task that lay ahead. 'Colonel Woodruff T. Sullivan, the senior officer, came to see me one day and saw the calendar. He asked to borrow it and that is how 'Project Emily' got its name'. It was a name that was used on both sides of the Atlantic when referring to the construction of the first bases for nuclear missiles in the free world. So the mystery as to how the RAF's brief entry into the missile era was revealed.

Meanwhile, as the missile bases were completed and came on stream, RAF crews were being given hands-on training in the United States, learning to maintain and operate the missiles. One month of classroom training at the Douglas Aircraft Company factory at Tucson, Arizona, was followed by two months' practical training at Vandenberg Air Force Base in California. At the completion of this training RAF crews undertook a live firing. The first actual launch by a British crew, codenamed Lion's Roar, took place on 16 April 1959.

This was indeed a crucial test for the whole Thor project. The Americans saw it as an opportunity to showcase Thor in front of the press, particularly the British press. One hundred and eighty-two invited media and dignitaries witnessed the occasion, having been given a comprehensive tour of US missile facilities and factories. To the enormous relief of the authorities the launch was a total success. One US Senator went on record as saying, 'This should be reassuring to Great Britain that the weapon they are going to get works!' Chapman Pincher, the *Daily Express*'s respected defence correspondent, cabled his news desk in London: 'The successful launch put the suspect Thor in an entirely different light. Far from being just junk, as the Socialists have claimed, I can testify that Thor is now a highly reliable weapon.'

Heading the RAF launch team for Lion's Roar was a 37-year-old squadron leader from Cardiff, Peter Coulson. He was presented with the launch key as a souvenir of the historic occasion, and he later became commanding officer of No. 98 (SM) Squadron based at Driffield. Gp Capt R.T. Frogley, the senior RAF officer at Vandenberg in charge of the RAF trainees, and later to become commanding officer of the whole Driffield Thor complex of launch sites, declared, 'Thor has now taken its place in the RAF's armoury.' Brig Godfrey Hobbs, Director of Public Information at the Ministry of Defence, was fulsome in his praise. 'This is a magnificent achievement and makes Britain a full partner in the missile field', he said. And Maj-Gen William H. Blanchard, commander of the USAF 7th Air Division based in the UK, who had been chief US adviser to the RAF on the Thor programme, declared, 'Now that trained RAF crews are becoming available and launch emplacements in England are being completed, we are nearing our goal.'

Writing on the experience in a restricted Air Ministry publication shortly after the launch, Sqn Ldr Coulson recalled:

Without doubt the longest five seconds in the author's experience took place between the illumination of an amber light, which indicated that the engines were about to start, and the development of the full 152,000 lb of thrust, which lifted the 65 ft missile from its launch mount. Smoke and flames at the emplacement almost blotted out the view on television, but immediately reports started to come in from the visual observers that lift-off was normal and that the missile was climbing into programmed limits. It is still doubtful whether the heavy reverberations in the control centre at this time were due to the terrific thrust developed by the engines or by the 50 occupants hopping up and down with joy. It can truthfully be said that the RAF has added another very good weapon to its armoury. All who took part in 'Operation Lion's Roar' are convinced that the Thor weapon system in the hands of the RAF will play a vital part with the manned aircraft in maintaining world peace through the deterrent.

A further seven launches by RAF crews under training followed between June 1959 and March 1960. Once the Thor bases became operational in England, these were supplemented by what were termed combat training launches. CTLs were launches of missiles which had stood for months in readiness on UK launch pads, and were then transported back to Vandenberg for test firing. Every three months during the lifetime of the missile force one Thor, selected at random, was flown back to America for test launch. The object was to prove that the missiles could stand outside, subject to the varied weather conditions of an English summer and winter, and then be transported back to the United States and successfully fired. It proved the robustness not only of the Thor as a weapon system, but also the effectiveness of the RAF's maintenance procedures. For the crews this was a reward for good service and an encouragement to further effort in the search for operational improvements. It proved the effectiveness of the drills and countdowns practised week by week on operational deployment. Out of eight test firings by RAF crews in training, and twelve combat launches by crews drawn from the launch pads of the Feltwell, Driffield, Hemswell and North Luffenham complexes, only two were unsuccessful. One training launch failed when the missile broke up, and one combat launch was aborted when the missile had to be destroyed after veering off course.

As the missile squadrons became operational, Thor officially became part of the deterrent force of Bomber Command. An operational policy document, issued in July 1959, put the missiles on a permanent state of readiness, manned continuously around the clock. A percentage of Thor missiles were to be maintained at fifteen minutes from launch, twenty-four hours a day, 365 days a year. Targeting of the missiles was to be controlled through the Bomber Command operations centre, and the V-force alert and readiness plan was to be amended to include the Thor force. In the middle of 1960, when all twenty squadrons became operational, this was followed by a further directive which demanded that initially the Thor force was to maintain 60% of its missiles at 'standby' or 'available', working eventually towards 75% guaranteed readiness. This level of readiness was to be effective throughout the year, including all public holidays – in effect an order to sustain a round-the-clock wartime stance during peacetime.

When the plans to base Thor in Britain were first drawn up it was considered that the nuclear warheads should be stored in a central secure location, and only be transported to the scattered launch pads when there was a threat that the international situation was deteriorating. This meant that if all the warheads for all twenty squadrons were kept under US control at Lakenheath it would take some fifty-seven hours to distribute them across the whole of the Thor fleet. If the nuclear nose-cones were stored at the four main wing complexes, this time gap would be reduced to around twenty-four hours. When US Senator Stuart Symington, a leading figure in the Democratic Party, on a briefing mission to the UK to study the Thor deployment, realised the extent this compromised the capability of Thor to react swiftly, he threatened to take his concerns back to the US Congress. Not surprisingly, the RAF, strongly backed by the Air Ministry, took a similar view, that operational readiness demanded that the warheads should be permanently fitted. Against this there were Government concerns over the additional risks of having the missiles scattered down the East of England permanently armed with megaton nuclear warheads. In particular, government scientists were worried at the possibility of an accidental explosion if a missile should be struck by lightning. Set against this was the view of the Joint Intelligence Committee that the Government would receive at the most only twenty-four hours' warning of a Soviet attack on the UK, and possibly far less. In such circumstances the Thor fleet without its warheads hardly represented a deterrent.

Senator Symington made quite a stir when he arrived back in Washington. He alleged that the missile base he had been visiting, Feltwell in Norfolk, was a 'sitting duck for sabotage', and he complained that he had found no fully operational missile base in England, although Congress has been assured missiles 'were sitting there ready to go'. He said that ten weeks after that statement had been made to Congress by General Twining, chairman of the US Joint Chiefs of Staff, there was still nothing ready to go. There was nothing that met operational standards; nothing adequately dispersed, and the entire installation was an easy target for saboteurs. He quoted an American officer who had told him that anyone with a 0.22 rifle, who was any kind of a shot, could destroy the missiles from the public road by puncturing the fuel tanks. 'These are the facts', he told the Senate Appropriations Committee. 'I think it is important that the American people know the facts and are not kidded as to what our retaliatory capacity is.' The Senator, possibly exaggerating for political purposes – he was a potential Presidential candidate – suggested this was 'a deliberate policy to conceal from the people the weakness of our situation and the ineptness of the Administration in correcting that weakness.' Probably to the satisfaction of the British Government, his comments appeared not to have been given any coverage this side of the Atlantic.

One further complication had to be considered. A crucial part of the Thor agreement, as far as the USA was concerned, was that the warheads would remain in American custody and control. The issue was raised with the US Secretary of State. The grounds being that it was hard to accept that a nuclear warhead, attached to a weapons system under the operational control of another nation, could be possibly considered in the exclusive custody of the US, particularly when the only American control was possession of one of the firing keys, the co-operating ally having the other. The Pentagon had initially given Congress an assurance that the custody of US nuclear weapons would be 'maintained and protected separate from the carrying vehicle'.

Despite these discussions, the RAF's and the Senator's views carried the day. In May 1960 the decision was taken to fit the nuclear warheads across the whole of the Thor force. This was followed by the directive from Bomber Command, already referred to, which laid down that the Thor squadrons were to maintain a proportion of missiles within tactical readiness at all times.

A memorandum to Air Marshal Sir Kenneth Cross, C-in-C Bomber Command, set out the launch procedure in stark terms:

The Air Ministry now have under urgent consideration the steps which are required to bring the political machinery into line with the readiness of the weapon. It is considered, however, that when the V-force are dispatched on 'positive control missions' the Thor force should be brought to T-8 [eight minutes to firing] and, should current research and development studies prove it practicable, a proportion of the force should be brought to T-2 [two minutes from firing and loaded with fuel]. There is, in fact, no difference in the problems with the two forces; when the decision is made not to recall the manned bombers, we must simultaneously commit the Thor force. It is one and the same decision.

When missiles were held in a vertical unfuelled condition, seven or eight minutes from firing, a large number of expensive components were required. Some sub-systems, which had a limited life, would be running continuously. The idea of holding a missile at around one-and-a-half to two minutes from launch was attractive. But this raised even greater problems. Once fuelled, the missile was designed to be held in that state no longer than two hours. After that, certain components became frozen through contact with the super-cold liquid oxygen. At this point propellants had to be pumped out, and a six-hour recovery period was needed to bring the missile back to an operational state. A technical trial at Vandenberg showed that the Thor force, after modifications, could be held at eight minutes to readiness without incurring too many extra running costs. But the routine readiness state was fifteen minutes from firing.

The opportunity of training in the States was attractive to RAF servicemen posted to an entirely new role for the service. Some regarded the introduction of ballistic missiles as the future for the RAF, a chance to get in on the ground floor of a new technical age which would eventually overtake the RAF's traditional flying role.

Junior Technician Ian Killick, who was posted to Feltwell, recalled his first impression on arriving at the Norfolk airfield. He asked himself what sort of operational unit this was. And why were American Air Force personnel present?

The morning after our arrival the Station Commander welcomed us on camp and made it clear that security would be of maximum importance as Feltwell was to be the first station to host Thor missiles. Sixty Thor missiles were to be deployed in the UK distributed between four RAF stations. Feltwell, the first to be equipped, was also to be home to the school for future training when the Americans officially handed over the weapon to all British crews. The engineering officer then explained what role this weapon would play

*in Bomber Command and what training we would have to undertake.
That this training would be in America boosted morale no end!*

The assignment looked even rosier when the first group from
Feltwell learned that the trip to the States would entail crossing
the Atlantic, there and back, in relative luxury by ocean liner.
In the late fifties RAF Air Transport Command was equipped with
the Hastings as its main troop carrier, and it had a limited fuel
capacity. A transatlantic flight would have meant going via Greenland and Canada for refuelling. So Ian Killick's crew, and others
who followed, were transported in old-style comfort. Killick and his
colleagues travelled in the *Carinthia* on the outward journey and a
French liner, the *Flandre*, for the trip back to the UK. Another former
Thor technician, Jack Gilchrist, who went on to become missile
servicing chief at RAF Catfoss in East Yorkshire, sailed for his
training course in the States on board the Cunard liner *Sylvania*,
and returned to the UK aboard the old *Queen Elizabeth*.

Once in the States, the crews faced a train journey of several days
to reach Arizona, where the Douglas Aircraft Company Missile
School was based in Tucson. Getting down to learning about
Thor, the RAF men found the programme demanding. Reveille at
4.50 a.m., breakfast at 5.20 a.m., technical lessons and study from
6.40 a.m. to 15.00 p.m., and lights-out in their accommodation no
later than 20.30 p.m.! There were some twenty individual training
courses, depending on which specialisation men were being trained
for. Some lasted just a few weeks, some up to three months.

Ian Killick's course was dealing with hydraulics and pneumatics.
'Although all the systems were new to us,' he remembered, 'a lot
of the components were familiar, so it was not like starting from
scratch, and we soon got into the learning routine.'

About a year after he had returned to Feltwell, following training in the States, Ian Killick was sent with a group of other Feltwell
personnel back to America for a test-firing exercise at Vandenberg.
By then, April 1960, Air Transport Command had been re-
equipped, and instead of the luxury of another transatlantic liner
they were flown to California in a Britannia transport aircraft. The
missile they were to launch had been brought back from England.

Mr Killick recalls, 'We were informed by the USAF authorities that orders to fire the missile would be given any time between 1 May and 4 May, and that it would be a daytime launch, so we had eight days to get the missile into position, check systems and get it into a T-15 state of readiness.' T-15 denoted fifteen minutes maximum between the order to launch and actual take-off.

Mr Killick continued,

Our normal working day was 7 a.m. to 5 p.m., with two half-hour and one hour-long breaks. The hours were long and the weather hot but working conditions were excellent and all the facilities first class, with plenty to eat and drink. It took six days to complete the task, giving us some breathing space before the first launch date. However, this was not always an advantage as it also gave time for things to go wrong. From the morning of 1 May everyone was on standby waiting for word to be given to prepare for a launch, but we had to wait until 11.30 a.m. on 2 May before orders were issued to start the countdown. This was when the adrenalin started to pump, and we were all hoping that no major faults would occur before the engine started. All went well to phase four when we were put on hold two minutes from launch. Someone at launch control obviously thought it added a bit of spice to the occasion by putting a hold on at such a late stage. With two minutes to go this was the last possible opportunity to stop the launch. From this point all systems on the missile went into internal power, guidance control took over and everything became automatic. It was part of the training to ensure the launch crew were in full control of what was a very dangerous piece of hardware.

Hold came off just after 12 noon, and at a few minutes past, to everyone's relief, engines started. The thing lifted off and thankfully went straight up! The flight was tracked by land-based stations and naval ships in the Pacific positioned near the programmed target area. They recorded where the nose-cone entered the sea, and this information was processed and the results reported back to launch control. The target area was 2 miles square and our shot landed 0.7 mile short and 1.2 miles right of the centre spot – very successful.

Sqn Ldr Frank Leatherdale, who commanded No. 220 (SM) Squadron at North Pickenham, Norfolk, from November 1959 to

February 1962, sailed for his training in the States on the *Mauretania* from Southampton to New York via Cherbourg and Cork. 'It was fascinating travelling on one of the great Atlantic ocean liners', he recalled. 'Despite her size there was some sea-sickness among the passengers as we encountered heavy weather. I remember losing the princely sum of half-a-crown on a bet of how far the ship had travelled in twenty-four hours.'

Frank Leatherdale said he found the training quite hard going, partly because of the new technical equipment they were trying to master and partly because the American method of instruction and their rather verbose technical manuals. Training was intensive and started at 4.45 a.m. every day. When the final exams came he was surprised to pass with 89%. 'Goodness knows how', he recalled. 'At the time the midday temperature in Tucson was around 104 °F, with oppressive humidity and thunderstorms most nights.' After watching two Thor launches at Vandenberg, one launched by an RAF team, and the other by the Americans, he returned to England in a civilian airliner to Stansted.

Jack Docherty, a launch-control operator, posted originally to Feltwell and later transferred to 98 (SM) Squadron at Driffield, was one of those sent for three months' initial training in the States. He recorded his experiences on 269 Squadron's website:

My batch of sixty trainees travelled to the US on the SS Ile de France, *an ex-German liner commandeered by the French as a war reparation. It was an elderly boat with fairly primitive accommodation, four or six bunks to a cabin, ventilation non-existent, one shower to ten cabins – but the catering was fantastic. Every meal was an* haute cuisine *experience. At each lunch and dinner place setting was a bottle of red and a bottle of white wine. The dining room and bar service was just so civilised. Nothing was too much trouble; there was no such thing as closing time. As long as you wanted service, they provided it. When we arrived at New York we were all several stones overweight and the boat dry of beer and spirits.*

American law prohibited all but US citizens access to US nuclear technology – the reason why on Thor bases in the UK USAF personnel had ultimate custody of the nuclear warheads and held the war/peace key for arming the warhead. So RAF trainees had to be inducted into the USAF as a way of temporarily circumventing US law.

Jack Docherty wrote:

> We attended an army base in Brooklyn to be sworn into the USAF and be issued with ID cards in the equivalent rank. The greatest advantage of having membership of both services was that the USAF paid us the difference between our RAF rank and our USAF rank. We had two pay days a week! After a week of amazement in New York – Times Square, Madison Square Gardens, Empire State Building, Irish bars, jazz clubs, etc. – we travelled from Grand Central Station to Tucson. The journey took four days via St Louis, Kansas City, Wichita, Amarillo and Alberquerque. For someone brought up on a diet of cowboy films and cowboy books it was a great experience.
>
> We were based at Davies Monthan Air Force Base, Tucson, and trained at the Douglas Aircraft plant there. The training was, initially, the theory of rocket engines, propellants, inertial guidance, ballistics and targeting. It was intrinsically very interesting but had to compete for our attention with the nightlife of Tucson and the nearby Mexican town of Nogales. Some people said that if it had not been for the lectures we would have had no sleep at all! Despite our apparent lack of attention we all did well in the exams taken after four weeks. The group then separated for further training in various specialisations: rocket engines, inertial guidance, etc. We operators moved on to Los Angeles for two weeks at the Douglas Aircraft production plant at Santa Monica to see the Thor manufacturing process. The most impressive aspect of this was seeing the aircraft production process. The plant was a vast arrangement of hangars with raw materials going in at one end, and a mile-and-a-half further on Globemasters rolling out at the other.

Jack Docherty spent the final six weeks of his training, like others in the RAF Thor squadrons, at the missile facility at Vandenberg Air Force Base, California. Vandenberg was a huge semi-desert site adjacent to an airfield, the main testing base for the US strategic missile programme. The missiles were above ground, but the control rooms were underground.

I was impressed by the professionalism and sense of urgency displayed by the USAF, Douglas and other company personnel working on the Thor project. There were now about twenty of us and we were assigned to a particular technical expert. I was assigned to an inertial guidance engineer. The task was to launch a pre-production missile – only the third Thor launch ever. One of the previous two had exploded on the launch pad, hence the underground control rooms. It was a case of working night and day to get all the components working correctly and at the same time – much like an aircraft really. I was particularly impressed by the complexity and precision of the inertial guidance system. It was an arrangement of stabilisation and accelerometer gyros whose role was to guide the rocket to a point on its launch parabola at a velocity that the warhead could be released and lofted on to its target. They reckoned they could 'drop it into a pork barrel at 1,500 miles'. The machining accuracy required of the inertial guidance system was of an entirely new order. Douglas Aircraft at first used aero engine machinists accustomed to working inside one-thousandth of an inch. They were now required to work inside a micron. The machine shops were like medical laboratories with machinists dressed like surgeons looking into microscopes at the job they were machining. The traditional machinists began to crack up with the stress of what they were attempting to do, so Douglas recruited 16-year-old schoolgirls who didn't know a micron from a hole in the head, showed them what to do and they just did it. After solving numerous technical problems we finally launched our missile with the sound of half a dozen Vulcan bombers. It landed within 100 yards of its target somewhere south-east of Hawaii. And so back to the UK. This time on the SS Liberté, another ex-German liner operated by the French. We were posted to RAF Feltwell, in Norfolk.

Jack Docherty went on describe that on arrival at Feltwell they found the missile site not yet built. McAlpine, the construction company responsible for the basic construction, had been on strike for some weeks and the site was being picketed by CND. Three months later the missiles were installed and the RAF crews were employed on missile commissioning. After 77 (SM) Squadron had become operational, a group of RAF personnel were returned to the USA for what was called 'integrated missile training'. This involved a further six weeks at Vandenberg for technical and operational training to launch another Thor, and once again there was transatlantic travel by cruise liner, this time on Dutch liners the SS *Statendam* and the SS *Rotterdam*. On his return to the UK Jack was posted to 98 (SM) Squadron at Driffield.

In fact Jack Docherty probably saw more of Vandenberg than most on the Thor force. In April 1959 a team of operational and technical personnel from Driffield and its satellite launch sites was formed to return to Vandenberg and carry out the first missile launch involving exclusively RAF personnel. This was the launch codenamed 'Lion's Roar'. On this occasion there was no luxury sea-trip. The group flew out on a Comet of Transport Command.

Jack Docherty recalls:

> At Vandenberg the RAF team took over the launch operations centre and readied the missile for launch. The control room was manned round the clock, at night by one of us launch-control operatives. There was a general warning to beware because a mountain lion was loose on the site. It had somehow found its way through the security fence and it was feeding off the deer which were plentiful roaming the site. It was said to be fierce because it had been very aggressive with an airman on an adjacent missile site. We were not allowed firearms because of the numerous RP-1 and liquid-oxygen tanks in the area. Throughout the night the duty LCO had to visit the launch pad to do hourly checks of temperature pressures, voltages and frequencies. The door to the control room was like a manhole cover. At 4 a.m. one day I emerged from the control room like a clanger surfacing on the moon just as the first light of dawn was breaking. Twenty yards in front of me was the mountain lion. It was huge and looked at me as if it was looking for breakfast. I shot back down the hole, slammed the lid shut and did not emerge again until the day shift arrived. I faked the readings. Despite the falsification of this vital data, the launch was a complete success. So once again we returned to the UK to resume normal operations.

During the short Thor era 1,200 RAF airmen were given missile technical training in the United States of America.

CHAPTER 9

War-ready, 24/7

When the Thor bases had been declared operational, RAF and USAF crews settled down to a routine of maintenance, training, exercising and ensuring security. Keeping the launch sites at fifteen minutes' readiness twenty-four/seven and sustaining a high level of morale was a massive undertaking. This was particularly true, because after the initial boost of training in the States, and of taking on a new and very different role compared to the RAF's traditional flying activities, life on the Thor bases could be thought of as pretty boring. On remote satellite launch pads many hours were spent cut off from all but telephone communication with the operations centre at the main wing head-quarters, reacting to exercise countdowns, and maintaining training routines. Keeping crews at round-the-clock peak of fifteen minutes' readiness under these conditions was no easy task. There was a tendency for some personnel from flying stations to denigrate the new missile squadrons. One former Thor NCO said: 'We were known by the rest of the Air Force as "The Penguin Squadrons" – all flap and no fly!' This was a reference to the continual count-down exercises but never a launch. The truth was that the missiles were kept at a similar state of readiness to the V-bomber force. But Thor had much less publicity. Its launch crews were not regarded as fulfilling the same glamorous role as colleagues stationed at the front-line V-force bases, and they were rarely if ever in the spotlight. Keeping a lid on publicity as far as possible was Government policy. But so was maintaining a new wartime deterrent stance.

One launch controller recalls:

Life was routine shift-work, practising launch countdowns, routine checking of missile systems and sitting at a missile console hoping war would not break out. Although the missiles sites were maintained and operated by RAF crews, there was considerable technical support from USAF personnel. All the messes were integrated and we had fun introducing the Americans to warm beer. We challenged them to a cricket match. They played it like baseball and hammered every ball over the horizon. They won by miles so they challenged us at baseball. They wiped us out again. So we gave up!

The Bomber Command Strategic Missile School was up and running at Feltwell from early 1961, and a parade took place in May that year to mark the handover of Thor missile training from the USAF to Bomber Command. Courses for launch-control officers, technical officers, authentication officers, missile service chiefs and missile electrical and general fitters were run as routine at Feltwell. The missiles had arrived from the States with surprisingly sketchy operational instructions. It fell to staff at Feltwell, as the first RAF complex to become operational, to rewrite the instruction manuals and produce standard operating procedures. They accomplished this so successfully that eventually the USAF themselves adopted the RAF's version.

There was ongoing emphasis on development training of launch crews. High priority was given to improving simulated launch procedures and refining the most effective ways of speeding up the countdown and launch process. Exercises were made as realistic as possible, ensuring crews were combat ready. In early 1960 the flowing of liquid oxygen into the missile was introduced as a normal part of countdown exercises. 'Wet' countdowns, as they were called, were pioneered at Feltwell in June.

Before that, countdowns had been carried out 'dry', without any propellant being pumped into the missile's tanks. The following month Feltwell pioneered a further stage, making countdowns

he first Thor ready for test firing at Cape Canaveral in January 1957. The launch was a disaster, the
missile failing to lift off. The first four test launches ended in failure. *(USAF)*

Removing the wreckage after the first Thor IRBM test at Cape Canaveral. A liquid oxygen valve failed almost immediately after lift-off and the missile slipped back to explode on the pad. Exactly two months after this disaster President Eisenhower and Prime Minister Harold Macmillan announced an agreement to deploy Thors in the UK. *(USA*

Lt Gen Bernard Schriever, Commander of the Western Development Division, the man put in command of the early US missile programme that resulted in the Thor IRBM and the later intercontinental range ballistic missiles that followed. He is pictured with (left) Trevor Gardner, Assistant Secretary of the Air Force for Research and Development and Dr Simon Ramo of the Ramo-Wooldridge Corporation. *(USA*

Before the launch sites were built in Eastern England during *Operation Emily*, the Douglas Aircraft Company created a mock up of an operational launch site with its accompanying tanks, power generators and control trailers close to their factory in Santa Monica.   *(Archant, Norfolk)*

September 1958. British and American officers greet the first Thor missile to be delivered to a UK launch site at RAF Feltwell in Norfolk.   *(Len Townsend)*

Working to tolerances as small as a hundredth part of a human hair, the Thor inertial guidance gyros are assembled in surgically clean conditions.   *(USAF)*

The Thor production line at the Douglas Aircraft Company's factory.   *(USAF)*

Thor in the village of Weldon (AF Pho

Manoeuvring Thor around narrow village streets and lanes in the east of England presented considerable problems. The missile with its transporter was ninety feet long and eleven feet six inches wide. This photo taken at Weldon, Northants illustrates the difficulties. *(USAi*

To assist the Thor convoys to negotiate narrow roads and sharp bends the original transporter design was modified to accommodate two steersmen seated either side of the missile close to the rear wheels. They were in contact by intercom with the driver of the hauling tractor, known as a 'Hippo'. *(USA*

noke and flames belch out as the first Thor launched
an RAF team begins to lift off and the full 152,000 lb
the thrust is delivered.   (USAF)

n Ldr Peter Coulson MBE, AFC at the launch control
nsole during the RAF's first Thor launch at
ndenburg Air Force Base, USA.   (USAF)

December 1958. Local police, supported by MoD police, line up at the gates of RAF North Pickenham to prevent intrusion by CND protestors while the launch sites were being built. *(Archant, Norfolk*

December 1958. CND demonstrators squat in the mire at North Peckenham in an attempt to prevent lorry load of cement being driven away to continue work on the building of the launch pads as part of *Operation Emily*. *(Archant, Norfolk*

typical Thor base layout. In the background two missiles stand erect on their pads. The third missile ready to be erected, its hangar having been slid back on its rails. Despite the solid blast walls, had he missile been fired in anger its launch pad would have been destroyed by the blast. This was uddenham in Suffolk, home of No 107 (SM) Squadron. *(Courtesy Sqd Ldr Frank Leatherdale)*

n aerial photograph of the launch pads (top left) at North Pickenham in Norfolk, home of No 220 M) Squadron . The runways and aircraft parking bays of this former USAF bomber base are still early visible. *(Courtesy Sqd Ldr Frank Leatherdale)*

Junior Technician Ian Killick at a Thor
technical console during training at the
Guided Missile School in the USA. He
was later posted to Feltwell in Norfolk
(Courtesy Ian Killick)

RAF technicians taking the Thor
propulsion course in the USA at
Rocketdyne, manufacturers of the
main engine system. (USAF)

Master Navigator Lachlan Brown in
radio contact with the missile control
caravan as the missile is made ready
for a practise launch sequence.
(Archant, Norfolk)

Master Pilot MH Sloane AFM at the launch control panel during Exercise *Lion's Roar*, April 1959.
(USAF)

16 April 1959, the first Thor launch by an RAF crew at Vandenberg Air Base in California, code named *Lion's Roar*. *(Len Townsend)*

Thor was designed to be air transportable and a massive airlift was required to bring sixty missiles and their associated equipment to their launch bases. Here one of the first Thors arrives at Lakenheath Air Base flown in by a C124 Globemaster.

(Ian Killick)

Every member of the RAF who attended the Thor Missile Training School at the Douglas Aircraft Company in Tucson received a certificate of training on completion of the course. Some 1,200 men were given training in the USA and subsequently at the RAF's missile training school at Feltwell in Norfolk.

(Courtesy Sqd Ldr Frank Leatherdale)

CERTIFICATE OF TRAINING
ON THE
THOR WEAPON SYSTEM

This is to certify that

has satisfactorily completed a course of training as indicated below in the United States Air Force IRBM (Thor) Weapons System. This acknowledgment is presented as a record of his proficiency in the skills required to support this Air Frame and Ground Support Equipment.

An RAF Chief Technician in the Electronics Trailer checks the dials and indicators to monitor the process leading up to the missile launch.

(Archant, Norfolk)

Inside a Thor launch trailer. An RAF launch controller (LCO) sits at the launch console, his finger on the key that initiates the launch sequence. Standing with his hand poised over the war/peace key that arms the nuclear warhead is the USAF authentification officer. Watching at his consol sits the RAF Master Navigator.
(Archant, Norfolk)

Thor could carry a 1.45 megaton nuclear warhead in just a few minutes from its English bases to Moscow and many other targets in the USSR. The Russians therefore made the bases prime targets. *(USAF)*

No 220 (Strategic Missile) Squadron at RAF North Pickenham, Norfolk on 3 May 1960. Each squadron in the Thor force consisted of five flights. One flight was always on duty and at immediate readiness to respond to orders to launch.
(Courtesy Sqd Ldr Frank Leatherdale)

A Thor crew with its technicians and security detachment (Flight) in front of their missile. Note the USAF Authentification Officer at the front left and the RAF Launch Control Officer on the right.
(Archant, Norfolk)

Once the Thor bases became operational in England, every three months a missile that had stood at immediate readiness in the British weather was randomly selected to be flown back to the USA for what was termed a 'Combat Training Launch'. Of twelve such launches only one was aborted when the missile veered off course. *(Courtesy Ian Killick)*

Avro Vulcans of numbers 27 and 83 Squadrons line up at Scampton in Lincolnshire in May 1961, prior to a *Mayflight* exercise designed to test the ability of Bomber Command to alert, scramble and disperse the V- Force and bring the Thor Force to heightened alert. *(Archant, Norfolk)*

A Thor nuclear warhead convoy ready to transport the warheads from a launch site in the east of England for maintenance by USAF technicians. The covered trailer carried the warheads and was always accompanied by US and RAF police, and a van equipped as a fire tender.   *(Courtesy David Bal*

RAF Feltwell 1958. The missile hanger (right) slides back to reveal the Thor in the prone position behind its blast walls. Each launch pad was floodlit, adding to its menacing appearance at night.
(Archant, Norfol

During the Cuban Crisis in October 1962 the entire Thor force was put on heightened alert. On most of the Thor bases the missiles were erected, fuelled with liquid oxygen, the target systems checked and countdown held at the end of Phase Three - minutes from firing.
(Courtesy Sqd Ldr Frank Leatherdale)

Thor being raised to its launch position. Note the nuclear warhead on the tip of the missile.
(Courtesy Sqd Ldr Frank Leatherdale)

Checking the flow of liquid oxygen into a missile on an RAF launch pad. The super-cooled LOX can be seen 'boiling off' as a vapour cloud. During the Thor era this was a common sight when 'wet flow' exercises were being carried out.
(Courtesy Sqd Ldr Frank Leatherdale)

North Pickenham in January 1963. Six months later, on 10 July, it was among the final group of Thor
bases to be deactivated. *(Archant, Norf*

The end of a mission. A Helmswell Thor is loaded for its return to the USA. *(US*

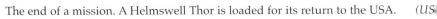

even more realistic. This involved a double propellant flow, fuelling the missile with LOX and pumping RP-1 simultaneously, a significantly hazardous operation. In July 1958 at Douglas's facility at Sacramento in Northern California, during a wet-flow test, a liquid oxygen pipe ruptured and the super-chilled liquid that had been frosting on the outside of the pipe instantly turned into a flaming inferno. Six men were seriously burned and three of them died. To reduce the chance of a similar accident, and to avoid the danger of an accidental launch, the RP-1 was flowed into a mobile tank beside the missile. Double-flow exercises were undertaken at each pad at least once per quarter to test crews under the most rigorous and realistic conditions. In the same way that Bomber Command examined and categorised aircrews, Thor launch crews were also regularly subjected to categorisation. Every nine months they were examined for operational efficiency by a command standards team. On-site assessment graded launch crews A, B or C for the coveted launch certificates. Anyone failing the categorisation was removed from operational duties and sent for retraining.

The danger of fire, when potentially hazardous liquids were being pumped from the storage tanks, meant fire precautions were rigid and fire-fighting drills routine. There was also, of course, the ever-present awareness that a live nuclear warhead was attached to each missile, although this was always replaced with a dummy warhead whenever exercises involving loading a propellant were undertaken. The initial fire-crew manning per squadron was strengthened in late 1960. A central 20,000 gal water storage tank was built at each satellite base to serve all three emplacements via a system of underground pipes serving strategic points on each pad. The system was pressurised by an electric pump capable of being switched on at any of the hydrants. Turning the water on immediately triggered a warning at the squadron guard-room and also at the main headquarters complex. Hoses were always pre-positioned, and monthly fire practice was mandatory at every site. Ernie Coppard, a launch-control officer based at Catfoss, near Hornsea in Yorkshire recalls:

Separately, the propellants were safe, but it was realised early on that the technical staff were in danger after liquid oxygen loading or top-up of the ground storage tanks. This danger was demonstrated to us by a safety team. An airman's jacket was dowsed with a cupful of LOX and left to 'dry'. After about ten minutes a lighted cigarette end was held at the end of a long cane close to the jacket. The blaze persuaded all smokers to air their clothes thoroughly after a loading and before smoking!

The liquid oxygen constantly evaporated, even though it was stored in insulated tanks. Sqn Ldr Frank Leatherdale, who was commanding officer of 220 (SM) Squadron based at North Pickenham in Norfolk, recalls that as LOX was so highly volatile every precaution had to be taken to ensure there was no risk of a spark from static or other electrical sources. Everything in contact with LOX had to be kept spotlessly clean. The LOX arrived in road tankers which had to be scrupulously washed down on arrival and earthed when the vehicle arrived at the launch pad.

The other fuel for use in the missile – RP-1 – was much safer to handle; nevertheless there were several safety precautions which had to be observed in its storage and handling. It had a tendency to stratify into layers with different specific gravities if undisturbed. So in the storage tank on the launch pad there was a paddle to agitate the fuel, and a heating coil to maintain it at the correct temperature and viscosity.

Fire was not the only hazard. Probably the most serious accident that occurred on any Thor site in the UK happened on 7 December 1960 at Ludford Magna, a satellite launch site of the Hemswell complex. A full load of several thousand gallons of liquid oxygen was spilled all over the launch pad. The LOX, stored at very low temperature, caused extensive damage to the concrete pad and the surrounding technical facilities. There were fears that the launch structure itself might become crystalline and that lowering the missile would constitute a danger. The accident could have had much more serious consequences; even so, the incident was regarded as such a major breach of safety rules that, following a full-scale inquiry, 104 Squadron's CO was replaced and Hemswell's station commander, a group captain, was required to hand over his command. Questions were asked about the incident in Parliament, and the Secretary of State for Air, Julian Amery, confirmed that the accident could have led to a very serious fire. He said,

> We maintain the highest standard of efficiency on stations of this kind, and where there is any fall-down in efficiency pretty strict measures have to be taken. There had been major deficiencies, not in the shape of an accident, but of other sorts at the station before, and in the circumstances the Air Officer Commanding thought the right decision was to recommend the posting of the commanding officer, and we have seen no reason to take another view.

There was some ill feeling over this decision. At the stage the liquid oxygen was about to be loaded into the missile the launch-control officer noticed an error, and a representative of the Douglas Aircraft Company, who was on site, was asked his advice. He said it was OK to proceed, and it was at this point the main LOX valve was opened and a vast quantity of LOX spilled all over the site. Ironically, although all three senior officers were reprimanded and posted away, the Douglas representative got off scot-free!

Keith Harris, who was a missile servicing chief, and before that a missile maintenance technician, at Feltwell recalls that on one occasion

> the 93 ft switch malfunctioned and the 'bird' tried to rise inside its shelter. It was just stopped in time by Ken Gault, the missile servicing chief. Ken was immediately stuck into the guard-room and despite his protestations accused of incompetence. The old tendency to blame the ground crew if anything went wrong was applied to our boss. The switch was faulty, as we insisted it was at the time, which led to a modification of all the 93 ft switches across the whole missile fleet.

The most serious safety concern was the possibility of an accident involving nuclear material, not only on one of the launch sites, but when nuclear warheads were being transported to and from bases and to and from a USAF airfield. The record of one Thor squadron states:

> Crews were trained in special safety drills associated with the warhead. In the event of an accident each man had a specific task to

perform, and these were practised regularly, both on the squadron and on a station basis. The exercises involved evacuation of the site, followed by radiation monitoring of the area. Area cordoning and decontamination drills were also practised.

It was a routine to check pads with Geiger counters to detect radiation leaks where missiles were armed with live warheads.

What precautions would have been taken to protect the civilian population in the event of a nuclear accident is not recorded, but would presumably have been the job of the police and the civilian fire brigades. At a press conference in February 1958 Duncan Sandys, the Minister of Defence, gave an assurance that there could be no accidental nuclear explosion at a Thor missile site. If there was a fire, he said, the main risk would be from detonation of a certain amount of high explosive. Such an explosion would be most unlikely to have an effect outside the circumference of the launch complex. In the unlikely event of a detonation, he added, there might also be some danger of radioactive contamination, which he thought would be localised and could be dealt with by simple decontamination procedures. He was at pains to emphasise that the nuclear warheads would be maintained in an unarmed condition and the arming process would not begin until the missile had actually been launched.

The Minister emphasised that if a missile went off course after launch there were arrangements for destroying it in the air.

There is doubt, however, that Sandys was correct in giving this public assurance. Len Townend, who was a missile maintenance technician based at Feltwell and was responsible for both helping to write the operational manual for launch crews and training crews, said:

As far as I know, and was trained to believe, as soon as the American authentication officer turned the war/peace key the warhead was armed. To me this always meant the warhead was active from that point. I know of no way the launch crew could have affected the missile in flight, but I suppose it could have been possible for us crewmen to be kept in the dark about this. I know for certain that the training I gave to crews always stressed that it would not be a sensible thing to be able to communicate with the missile after it left the launch pad. If we could do it, so could the enemy, and anything we launched could then be easily neutralised. We were not playing at war games; if we launched Thor we knew World War Three had started.

Mr Townend added:

The RAF had no access to the warhead or its control system. They were totally under the control of the USAF. However, when we fired a missile for training launches in the States, obviously without an armed warhead, the USAF ground controller could destroy the missile at any time. They would not have wanted an errant missile to fall somewhere it could cause damage. All training Thors were fitted with an explosive collar which, if detonated by a radio signal, blew the thing apart. This device was fitted by USAF technicians only a few hours before the training launch. But this system was most certainly not active on operational missiles in the UK.

The only fail-safe on the operational missiles standing at launch pads down the East of England was the warhead-arming process. The initial arming act, that opened the necessary circuits, was the turning of the war/peace key by the American authentication officer in the last phases of the launch. The final arming of the weapon was triggered by the warhead's separation from the rest of the missile as it reached the requisite point in its trajectory to deliver it towards the target.

The CO of one of the four complexes of launch sites recalls that the nuclear warheads had to be moved frequently to and fro between the headquarters site and the dispersed launch pads. This entailed conveying the warheads on public roads with all the attendant dangers of collision or breakdown. Given the distances between sites – in East Anglia it could involve trips of forty or fifty miles – there was a certain risk to the civilian population. Control of the warhead remained with the Americans, except when being moved by road, when it became an RAF responsibility, presumably because of Government concerns that the RAF should appear to be in charge. The former commanding officer recalls:

Such movements were done discreetly but the civil police and fire services were kept informed. Such convoys, unless done covertly, would have attracted demonstrators and the press, but I do not believe this ever happened at any of the Thor bases. They were quite safe from detonation, but if they had been involved in a serious accident which fractured the casing there might have been spillage of radio-active material which would be confined to a relatively small area.

Security on the Thor bases was a constant concern. There were fears of sabotage, and not only from covert Soviet agents. The RAF and the police were aware that so-called Eastern Bloc 'diplomats', in truth undercover Soviet agents of the GRU, the intelligence directorate of the Soviet military, paid considerable attention to the launch bases. The British authorities monitored their activities closely. When erected, a missile could easily have been put out of action by a well-aimed shot piercing the missile's outer skin. That was the reason why the activity of local farmers in the shooting season was carefully watched. Hostility of a section of the British public to the nuclear missiles showed itself in the form of marches and demonstrations organised by the Campaign for Nuclear Disarmament. CND had been formed in 1958, just when the first Thor missiles were arriving in England. Some of the demonstrations at bases being built in the East Anglian country-side became quite violent when police and construction workers used robust measures, as described in the last chapter. The declared policy of CND, however, was always peaceful demonstration.

The launch sites were not easy to access or infiltrate. They were closed off with a double 8 ft high security fence. High-intensity lighting illuminated them day and night, and they were patrolled twenty-four hours a day by RAF police and guard dogs. All squadron personnel were aware of the constant need for security. Taking photographs anywhere near the sites was strictly banned.

The late Gp Capt Roy Boast, who was in command of the Hemswell Wing, described the security arrangements at each launch site in a letter written in 1998:

The sites were surrounded by an eight-foot fence topped with three coils of barbed wire. There was a sterile area surrounded by three coils of barbed wire, one coil resting on the other two which were side by side. The whole area was kept close cut and was floodlit. There were policemen and a vehicle on duty at all times with two dogs and handlers patrolling an irregular pattern inside the site and the sterile area. There were three observation platforms on each site giving a good line of sight.

Security was regularly tested. Attempts were made to breach the launch sites by intruders from other squadrons. A history of No. 98 Squadron based at Driffield says the base was initially provided with

a so-called unclimbable fence, but security teams from No. 2 Police District mounted mock raids and soon proved this to be a fallacy. A roll of barbed wire was mounted atop the fence round the entire perimeter, and a triple roll of wire was coiled to a height of 4/5 ft inside the fence. This slowed down the speed of entry into the site and our police were successful in foiling the majority of 'raids'. Each launch crew had a sergeant and two corporal policemen, augmented at night by an establishment of five dog handlers. They also had a radio-equipped Land Rover and two pack-sets, and continuous patrols were mounted throughout the twenty-four hours. There were periodic threats from 'nuclear disarmers' but the squadron site was never breached and the police continued their lonely vigil with commendable enthusiasm.

Sometimes, however, 'intruders' from a neighbouring base were successful in gaining unauthorised entry. A squadron leader and a flight lieutenant from No. 106 (SM) Squadron based at Bardney in Lincolnshire concealed themselves in a missile checkout trailer before it was due to be moved from Bardney to Hemswell. They achieved their purpose and gained access to the Hemswell site without difficulty. The operational record book of Hemswell noted that the lesson had been learned and action had been taken to ensure this type of intrusion could not be successfully accomplished again.

Group Capt Boast, recalling the exercises to test security, wrote:

One evening I joined the police team in an exercise involving Hemswell and its dispersed sites. They provided me with a heavy-

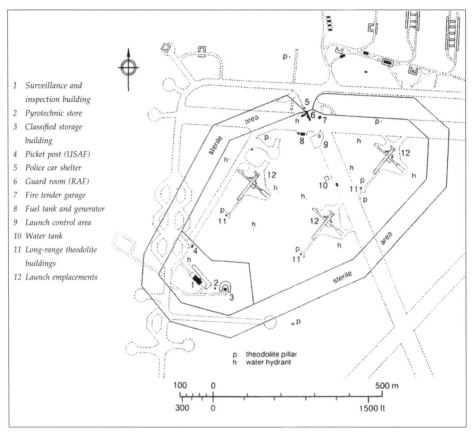

1 Surveillance and
   inspection building
2 Pyrotechnic store
3 Classified storage
   building
4 Picket post (USAF)
5 Police car shelter
6 Guard room (RAF)
7 Fire tender garage
8 Fuel tank and generator
9 Launch control area
10 Water tank
11 Long-range theodolite
   buildings
12 Launch emplacements

p: theodolite pillar
h: water hydrant

100   0   500 m

300   0   1500 ft

RAF Driffield, East Riding of Yorkshire. Plan of Thor main station emplacement area. (*Redrawn from NA AIR 27/2804*)

duty suit of denim, thick leather gloves, heavy boots and a woolly hat. We lay down in a turnip field just outside the main base squadron, and in thirty minutes we had a good idea of the security patrol pattern. As this was a random pattern we decided not to attempt there but try our luck elsewhere. At Coleby Grange the pattern was more regular so we decided to try and get in. I had assumed that I would stay outside and watch the policemen in action, but they persuaded me to crawl through the coiled wire into the sterile area. I was shocked to find out how easy it was, provided one did it slowly and carefully. I was even more shocked when we reached the perimeter fence, where I was hoisted onto one man's shoulders and was flung upwards and rolled over the coiled wire on top of the fence. I found myself inside the site, where I was quickly joined by one of the others. We ran towards the nearest missile shelter, but before we were halfway there we were confronted by a dog and his handler. Other policemen came running and the security vehicle sped round the sterile area to catch the other two intruders. After identity had been established, we conducted a debriefing over hot coffee.

Sqn Ldr Leatherdale recalls:

Our security at North Pickenham was always being tested by teams of RAF policemen from RAF Feltwell who were known as 'intruders'. They were well trained and practised in getting over the fences. It was quite surprising to see how agile they were. If the intruders were seen in the vicinity of the site a warning was broadcast over the Tannoy so that men working at the pads could be extra vigilant. But this very warning system also alerted the intruders to the fact that their presence had been noted, and so they would proceed with added caution. I devised a scheme whereby we would broadcast the message 'Coffee is now being served in the LCT'. Any Thor trained personnel would know that we would never allow liquids into the launch-control trailer for fear of spillage getting into any of the electrical circuits. I was upset when the next pair of intruders were caught and said with a smile, 'Please may we have our coffee now.' Obviously someone – probably one of our own RAF policemen – had told them of our ruse.

The Americans who controlled the storage and maintenance of the nuclear warheads were armed and obviously very security conscious. Dave Bale, who was an MT fitter stationed at Driffield, recalls how on one occasion he was sent to No. 98 Squadron launch pads to attend to an unserviceable fork-lift truck. He had forgotten his code number for the new security PIN system in use. The RAF policeman knew him and let him into the launch pad compound. However, the truck was stuck inside the American site where the nuclear warheads were kept. 'The US air police staff sergeant, a very large negro, would not let me in', he says. 'I asked him what he would do if I walked in. He replied he would shoot me. I believed him, so I left it to them to push the truck out so I could fix it.'

Capt Kenneth Moll, a USAF authentication officer based at Caistor in Lincolnshire, says he thought that in comparison to USA-based intercontinental missile sites, which were in underground silos and equipped with advanced sensing devices, the Thors were 'pitifully insecure'. 'They were potentially exposed to small-arms fire from outside and to attack by squad-sized groups.' Perhaps this was why the RAF and Ministry of Defence were sensitive about Eastern Bloc 'diplomats' travelling by car anywhere in the East of England. Some former RAF Thor personnel recall instructions to lower erected missiles when suspicious black limousines were seen in the area. A number of launch sites were quite close to public roads.

The Cold War reality in the 1960s was that a Soviet first-strike could take place with little or no warning. That was particularly true before the inception of the radar domes at Fylingdales in Yorkshire, a vital link needed to bring the American BMEWS (Ballistic Early-Warning System) on stream. When it became operational in 1963 it could spot incoming missiles over the horizon almost as soon as the Russians had fired them. But even the warning window provided by BMEWS gave only a matter of minutes in which Bomber Command could react: this became the famous four minutes warning. To keep launch crews in a state of continuous war readiness to respond immediately required strict discipline, dedication and constant exercises. In an alert situation literally seconds counted. Different categories of exercises under codenames Mayshots, Responds, Reclaims, Redoubles and Nightchecks were regularly sprung on the Thor force. Some were major Bomber Command 'no notice' readiness exercises to co-ordinate the alertness of both the V-force and the Thor force. Others were instigated at a lower level. Triplox, for instance, was an exercise designed to test the capability of a strategic missile squadron's launch crews to complete propellant loading at all three missile emplacements simultaneously. To those who lived in the vicinity of Thor bases the only visible sign of these exercises was that missiles could be seen raised to the vertical launch position. If liquid oxygen was being flowed into the missiles a telltale cloud of LOX could be seen billowing from them. No doubt for some of the public the sight of LOX 'boiling off' was pretty alarming.

A major exercise could even be disturbing for experienced officers in the Thor force. Sqn Ldr Frank Leatherdale, like other Thor squadron commanders of satellite launch sites, lived in a house close to base. He remembered:

Sometime in the autumn of 1961 I heard the klaxon on Pad 13 sounding, indicating that the shelter was moving back; nothing unusual about that. But then I heard another klaxon sounding, indicating that one of the other pads was also starting a countdown. I decided to go to the launch-control trailer to see what was happening, and as I did so the third pad started a countdown. We had twice before had simultaneous countdowns on all three pads, but it was unusual. When I reached the LCT the launch-control officer told me we had been instructed to carry out wet countdowns on all pads. Now this was the first time for all three Thors to be fuelled at once. I queried the order with the missile controller at RAF Feltwell, who assured me that the Bomber Command controller had ordered simultaneous wet countdowns throughout the Thor force and that we were to get our missiles to the fifteen-minute readiness state and hold them there. At that time the Cold War had warmed up a bit and the political situation was quite tense, with Russia rattling its sabres over Cuba.

We had been at fifteen minutes' readiness for some while and we were wondering how long it would be before we were told to de-fuel our Thors, because once they were erect and fuelled the LOX boiled off quite appreciably, and to get them back to a ready state would require the LOX storage tanks to be topped up again, which in turn would require British Oxygen to send in road tankers. Again I queried the situation with our controller, but he knew no more than we did.

It was a fine sunny morning, and just then we heard jet aircraft approaching from the west. Looking up I saw a number of parallel contrails heading straight out to the east. In my previous job at RAF Upwood I had known SACEUR's strike plan and knew how the Canberra force would be deployed in the event of war with Russia. I was horrified to see this plan apparently being implemented. Just then we heard the engines of the V-force bombers at RAF Marham start up, and the aircraft take off. I could only conclude this was IT. I was more than worried, I suppose I was rather frightened, but I had to maintain a calm face for my men. Quite apart from the threat poised by any Russian attack, there was always the risk of one of our own Thors failing to launch correctly and causing a nasty accident on its pad.

That apart, what would I tell my men when we had fired our IRBMs? Most lived in married quarters built in North Pickenham village. I decided I would send them home so that they could be with their families. Once our Thors had been fired there was nothing for the men to do as you could not re-use an operational Thor launch pad. The blast from the engine's exhaust would burn all the equipment around the pad, which was designed quite differently from the launch pads in use at USAF Vandenberg, which were built so that they could be re-used fairly quickly by dowsing the pad with a huge quantity of water just before main engine ignition.

After what seemed an eternity we received the order to de-fuel and lower our missiles. I must say I was quite shaken by this event, which turned out to be a very-full-scale exercise of our war role. At the time I had visions of Neville Shute's On the Beach, *which dealt with the aftermath of a nuclear war, coming to reality. Later on, when I could discuss the exercise with colleagues, I realised that this was part of the price of living close to a nuclear deterrent weapon system. Although I had, from childhood, always had a belligerent mind I never did get used to the psychological strain imposed by commanding a Thor squadron.*

In the eyes of Air Marshal Sir Kenneth 'Bing' Cross, C-in-C Bomber Command, the objective of these exercises, and the intense ongoing training that accompanied them, was to integrate the strategic missile force with the V-force and to maintain Britain's deterrent on permanent quick reaction alert. Cross' predecessor as C-in-C Bomber Command, Air Chief Marshal Sir Harry Broadhurst, who completed his term as C-in-C in May 1959, was less enamoured with the concept of nuclear missiles. Writing to the Deputy Chief of Air Staff in February 1958 he stated: 'The V bombers present a relatively simple problem because having brought them to readiness, I can order them off at the first warning, but I am still left with well over an hour in which to obtain a decision as to whether they should carry on and complete their attack or be recalled to base. On the other hand, as I see it, we will need two Governments to agree before the IRBMs can be fired but even then they could not be launched at first warning. This could only be done when the radar plots were definitely identified as hostile or, what is much more likely, after the Soviet bombs or missiles had started to fall on this country. In sum, it seems to me that given the same state of readiness i.e fifteen minutes, whereas the V bombers can be controlled through our present chain of command the IRBMs present an entirely different problem because the military readiness and the political decision to fire must coincide if we are to avoid having our 'deterrent' destroyed before it can be launched. I do not know how much thought has been given to this problem but I do urge most strongly that we know exactly what we are aiming at before we commit ourselves to any agreement with the Americans on a specific operational set-up.'

Within Bomber Command the relevant V-bomber alert states were 'Bravo' – the bomber force ordered to disperse; Readiness State Blue – V-force to come to forty minutes from take-off; Readiness State Red – V-force to fifteen minutes' readiness; and Scramble – which could be activated any time after Alert Alpha had been ordered. Alpha indicated to the Thor bases that the order to launch was imminent. A substantial proportion of the missiles were essentially at a permanent State Red. By modifications, and increasing the efficiency of the countdown, the time from initiation of the launch process to launch could be reduced. This drive to reduce the countdown was known as Operation Consolidate, and consisted of a series of modifications to the missiles and to ground equipment which led to the countdown sequence being speeded up. In general about forty, or two-thirds, of the Thor force missiles were maintained at constant readiness, ten were within six hours of readiness (probably undergoing routine maintenance) and the remainder within twenty-four hours or less. On receipt of an alert order, the maximum possible number – fifty to fifty-five missiles – were to be brought to the point of immediate initiation of a countdown. *In extremis*, and this appears, according to the recollections of launch crews, to have been the point reached at the height of the Cuban missile crisis, for a proportion of the Thor force the fifteen minutes to firing was further reduced to seven or eight minutes (in RAF parlance T-8). This was achieved by starting the countdown and holding it after completion of Phase Two of the five launch phases. It cut the firing time by a precious seven minutes. At this point the missile was ready to be pressure-fuelled with RP-1 and liquid oxygen.

A further step was practised, which held the launch at the end of Phase Three (T-2), at which point the missile was erected and filled with liquid oxygen and was between one-and-a-half and two minutes from launch. However, it was not possible to hold Thor safely at this hazardous stage for long, as there was a danger of the relief valve freezing from the extremely low temperatures of the LOX. Also, the liquid oxygen would continuously 'gas off' like a cloud of mist surrounding the missile, and consequently it required constant topping-up of the LOX in its tanks. If a high proportion of the Thor force were held at T-2 it would have imposed a serious national drain on available stores of LOX.

Reducing the countdown time certainly increased readiness, but it involved compromises. Keeping missiles in the vertical unfuelled condition (T-8) for any substantial length of time resulted in the need to replace a number of expensive components of sub-systems, which had limited life if they were kept running continuously. Keeping the missile erect and fuelled raised further component problems. After two hours loaded with LOX, parts of the missile were in danger of becoming frozen through contact with the super-cooled liquid oxygen. When that happened the propellant had to be pumped out, and it took six hours to recover the missile to its ready state. Modifications were made to overcome some of these problems, and during the latter stages of its deployment in the UK a trial at Vandenberg proved that the force could be kept at T-8 without incurring significant additional costs.

Len Townend, who was a missile servicing chief at Feltwell, described the launch procedure in characteristic style:

Thor rested in a horizontal position underneath a protective metal hangar termed as a shelter, which was mounted on railway-type tracks. The shelter was surrounded by a number of wheeled trailers which housed all of the complex gear required to keep the beast happy. A high-pressure nitrogen tank, two fuel-storage tanks (one rough-cut jet fuel and one liquid oxygen) completed the set-up for each bird.

The birds on one site were controlled by a single launch-control trailer (LCT). Electrical power was provided by four motor generator sets also mounted in wheeled trailers. However, it was recognised that if these generators were run twenty-four hours a day they wouldn't last long, so they were in place only as standbys and only used on exercises. Power was taken from the national grid through special converters on site [Thor ran on 60-cycles electrics – the British grid is 50 cps].

Now the bird, and what it did: it carried a nuke at the sharp end and three rocket engines at the blunt end. Two more rockets were mounted halfway along the thing. The main engine drove the missile at what can only be described as a hell of a rate. The main engine also did most of the steering (it swivelled). The two small engines at the back (Verniers) helped steer the bird on its final stage to an accurate point in space ('donut in the sky', as the Yanks insisted on calling it!). The two mid-engines (retro-rockets) were used to separate the rocket body (they were mounted pointing backwards) from the warhead when the moment of truth arrived, which thank the Lord it never did, although I wet my socks during Kennedy's Cuban do!

Launching the beast was quite a do. It was supposed to take fifteen minutes from 'Go-man-go' to being a ball of fire above the skyline, but training reduced this time to much less. On the command 'go' the mystic launch key (British) was turned and the whole process began (almost automatically) in five phases:

Phase One: Was an automatic electronic checkout of all missile systems. If this was OK the shelter rolled back on its tracks to leave the bird exposed to wind and rain (and the missile maintenance technician to get wet!)

Phase Two: The missile was automatically bolted to a launch mount, which then hinged through 90 degrees, power being provided by an enormous hydraulic cylinder.

Phase two consisted of raising the bird from its sleeping position to vertical. If you remember what Thor looked like you will know *why, during this phase on training launches, the married-quarters wives longed for their husbands to come home. When the bird was vertical, electric motors automatically unscrewed the three holding-bolts out of the missile.*

Phase Three: Things began to get serious in this phase, as about 10,000 gallons of fuel/oxidant was pushed into the bird in about eight minutes. The noise during this phase was pure Hollywood – screams, howls and grunts as the super-cold liquid oxygen bent the pipes all ways and put a layer of ice all over the bird.

Phase Four: Just a bit of mucking about on final electronic checks and topping up the fuel to the exact amount needed to hit the target. The USAF officer turned the war/peace key to arm the warhead during this phase.

Phase Five: Light the blue touch-paper and go! (Oh, the missile maintenance technician would have started running at the end of Phase Three, and by this time would be about five miles upwind – which wasn't too bad, considering end of Phase Four to lift-off was less than a minute.

The bird rose vertically to about 80,000 feet. It then rolled over and went hell-for-leather for the donut in the sky, which by juggling of the engines from an on-board computer put the thing in the right place to throw the nuke into an arc (like aiming a catapult), which would drop it on the planned city. The warhead and the rocket body then parted company (aided by the retro-rockets), the body breaking up and falling to the ground or sea.

The Thor missile, when not fuelled, was relatively fragile. It had a thin outer skin, and in transporting it care had to be taken not to dent or damage the outer casing. When fully fuelled it weighed 110,000 lb, but of this some 98,500 lb was fuel. Sqn Ldr Frank Leatherdale recalls that the Rocketdyne engine would generate 152,000 lb of thrust, but as it burnt its fuel very quickly the thrust developed soon far exceeded the missile's weight, and it would start to rise, slowly at first and then accelerate ever faster as the thrust-to-weight ratio altered. By the time the warhead separated from the main body it was travelling at more than Mach 10.

CHAPTER 10

Rural Convoys

The arrival of Thor caused some difficulties when it came to delivering the 65 ft missiles to some fairly remote locations down country roads and lanes. The missile was attached to its launch cradle, and hauled by a Leyland six-wheeled tractor. Together they formed a lengthy and by no means easily manoeuvrable articulated vehicle. When the missiles first arrived at Lakenheath a series of mock road layouts was created in a remote part of the airfield to practise the journeys the missiles would have to take. Oil drums and aircraft wheel chocks were used to simulate road widths and tight corners. After a deal of experimentation it was agreed it was necessary to get permission from the local authority for a certain amount of road widening. In places steel planking was used to ease the passage of the transporter-erector-launcher (TEL). Thor's erection spine, the structure that raised it into its firing position, doubled as its carrying trailer. It originally had been designed with a fixed rear axle, but the manufacturers, the Food Machinery and Chemical Corporation in Northern California, were asked to equip TELs for delivery to the UK with additional rear-wheel steering. Two steersmen were seated either side of the missile close to the rear wheels. This improved the manoeuvrability considerably. But it still became necessary for the Department of Transport to survey the routes between the main bases and the satellite launch sites, and in some instances carry out work to iron

out the worst bends. On the road it was an impressive sight. The
tractor, commonly known as a 'Hippo', and the missile attached
to its articulated trailer were some 90 ft long and 11 ft 6 in wide.
Although equipped with power steering, the tractor had a very
limited turning circle. The driver was able to talk by intercom to
the two driver/steersmen on each side of the rear bogie, but it was
still often necessary in some parts of the East of England, where
roads were particularly difficult to negotiate, to remove some road
signs, and adapt roundabouts to get the missiles to their firing
positions. One driver remembers that at a corner the rear steersmen would steer the tail out of the bend so that the trailer did not
cut in. 'Having said that,' he recalled, 'there was an occasion when
the rear steersman forgot, turned the wrong way and collided with
a post office!'

Another former RAF driver remembered the missiles arriving
by air in Globemaster aircraft. In his case he was involved in their
collection from RAF Scampton.

> We had to take two cranes, a tractor and transporter/erector with
> an American crew plus RAF police escorts. This was quite a
> performance as the missile had to be lifted off its cradle on which it
> had rested during the flight and onto the transporter/erector trailer.
> There were, of course, safety switches to ensure that the clamshell
> clamps for the nose and the securing clamps for the tail did not come
> apart en route. If the switches did not mate properly the vehicle
> brakes could not be released. Naturally, we had one on which the
> brakes could not be released no matter what the technicians did, so in
> desperation they disabled the system and in near-darkness we finally
> crept off.

The same individual remembered the first moves of a missile to its
launch site:

> In Market Rasen we had a right-hand turn from the main road to
> get into the Bardney launch site. The turn was a little tight and
> necessitated a bit of reversing. We caused a number of hold-ups
> there! Thankfully British Leyland vehicles, modified for our use,
> began to arrive and replace American vehicles. They were a bit more

powerful, with a tighter turning circle but no power steering. We all developed massive biceps! The convoy would consist of an RAF police vehicle, the missile, a crew bus for technicians and then another RAF police escort, so you can imagine we created quite a stir travelling through the local villages.

Squadron commanders had to act as convoy commanders when it was necessary to move a Thor to wing headquarters for a full service. One squadron leader recollects that these convoys would consist of the transporter-erector with its huge tug vehicle, a fire engine, two RAF police motor-cyclists, a Land Rover for the convoy commander, an RAF police radio vehicle and sometimes an ambulance as well. The country roads had to be cleared of other traffic at bends, hence the police motor-cyclists, and the convoy needed right of way at crossroads.

Continuing his recollections, the former RAF driver recalled,

The warhead and guidance nose-cone travelled separately on a specially modified trailer provided with a power supply to maintain the guidance-system temperature so the gyros did not topple. The trailer also had soft suspension so as not to jar the equipment, and an absolute speed limit of twenty miles an hour was imposed. The trailer was towed by a standard RAF three-ton truck. The convoy was similar to the missile itself, but as the trailer was bright yellow it caused a particular stir.

The Government's sensitivity that deployment of American missiles, albeit painted with RAF roundels, would be seen by the public as a US takeover, was shown by the fact that all US vehicles were repainted RAF blue before being taken on the public roads. American personnel travelling with them were ordered to dress in civilian clothes.

The dispersed squadrons, usually many miles distant from the wing headquarters complex, meant that the Thor force relied heavily on transport services, far more than any other type of RAF unit. No personnel lived on the dispersed launch sites, although in some locations council houses in nearby villages accommodated some of the married men and their families. In the main, however, most Thor crews lived at the headquarters complex, so Bedford buses were used to provide a shuttle service at each shift change and also to take specialist technical teams to perform other than routine maintenance. Gp Capt Roy Boast, who was CO of the Hemswell launch complex of bases, remembers that in one year his transport services clocked up at least half a million miles.

Dave Bales recalls that at Driffield

there was a fleet of 35 or so Morris J2 vans, which apart from dismal handling due to being front heavy had the lousiest gear change known to man. Nevertheless they were worked hard and ran up very high mileages. Most of them suffered a broken column gear-change fork within a week. We made our own by the dozen and could change them within seconds.

Some of these vans were used to take a pair of service policemen and their dogs to each site for security patrols round the perimeter fences. The bench seat remained behind the driver's bulkhead and a pair of cages were fixed inside the rear door to accommodate the dogs. Dave Bale again: 'These vans did return journeys to each remote site at 4 p.m., 11 p.m. and 6 a.m., and ran up very high mileages in their three years on the unit. They also stank to high heaven from the dogs!'

As well as towing the missiles on their transporters, the Leyland six-wheeled tractors were used daily to tow trailers transporting long cylinders of GN2 gaseous nitrogen. There was a daily run from Driffield of three empty trailers to BOC Leeds, with three full trailers in return. This meant a total of at least nine in transit, and this level of supply journeys was repeated at the other Thor complexes. Another task was to tow liquid oxygen tankers to the main suppliers for refilling, and take them out to the launch sites to replenish the missile tanks. One former driver based at Hemswell remembered that leaving Brinsworth, where the liquid oxygen was collected, the unit had to climb a long hill: 'Our tractors were only just man enough for the job. Halfway up the hill was a newsagent, and the observer in the cab would nip off the tractor, across to the shop for a newspaper and be back to climb back on before we had gone very far, such was the slow speed using a crawler gearbox.' These kinds of journey were being repeated across the whole of the Thor force squadrons – a major transport undertaking to keep all launch sites supplied. There were also regular convoys moving live nuclear warheads to and from the various bases. These convoys were a regular sight, and although movement of warheads was undertaken with high security they certainly could not escape the notice of local people. The giveaway was that they were always prominently guarded by RAF and American police and shepherded by a fire appliance.

CHAPTER 11

'Quick Reaction Alert'

From November 1957 RAF Bomber Command and America's Strategic Air Command agreed to work together to produce a fully integrated target policy. In joint RAF/USAF discussions, with input from the Air Ministry, it was clear that by pursuing separate strategies the two air forces would reduce their joint impact, because they each planned to strike many of the same targets. A strategy was agreed that maximised the strike forces available to the two commands, taking into account the RAF's ability to be on target first in the initial wave, several hours before the main Strategic Air Command aircraft could reach targets in the Soviet Union or the Warsaw Pact countries from their bases in the US. The plan also took into account nuclear-armed American aircraft operating from UK bases in East Anglia.

A confidential memorandum from the Chief of the Air Staff stated:

Under the combined plan, the total strategic air forces disposed by the Allies are sufficient to cover all Soviet targets, including airfields and air defences. Bomber Command's contribution has been given as 92 aircraft by October 1958, increasing to 108 aircraft by June 1959; 106 targets have been allocated to Bomber Command as follows:

69 cities, which are centres of government or of other military significance, 17 long-range air force airfields which constitute

111

part of the nuclear threat, and 20 elements of the Soviet air defence system.

It is intended that a third meeting will be held this month to co-ordinate the actual routes, timing and tactics of the aircraft attacking the targets selected. Full tactical co-ordination of operations will thus be achieved. In addition to the co-ordination of war plans, Bomber Command and SAC are also studying such measures as the use of each other's bases, the integration of intelligence, warning, and post-strike recovery. Arrangements have also been agreed between the RAF and USAF to co-ordinate the Thor strike capability as this becomes effective. This, of course, is particularly important in view of the very short time of flight of these weapons.

Britain became an independent thermonuclear power in February 1958 with the delivery to RAF Wittering in Cambridge-shire of the first high-yield fission weapon, codenamed Violet Club. It was very much an experimental stop-gap weapon, and alarmingly was inherently unstable. The Government sanctioned its delivery to the RAF to prove, at the first possible date, the UK's thermonuclear capability. Although its development programme was incomplete, it now appears that corners were cut and it was deployed under some severe strictures, despite concerns expressed by the Controller of Armaments at the Ministry of Supply. In their book *Planning Armageddon*, Stephen Twigge and Len Scott assert that at the time of its deployment the operational effectiveness and safety of the weapon was in some doubt.

As Violet Club took a minimum of 30 minutes to prepare it could not be placed on quick reaction alert unless safety measures were relaxed. Once the safety device was extracted from the weapon, it immediately became live.

The warhead contained enough Uranium 235 to form an un-compressed supercritical mass, so it was feared that if a mechanical deformation occurred, a small explosion or an accident in which the weapon was dropped could result in a full-yield nuclear explosion.

The fact that a further five of these weapons were assembled on Bomber Command stations across East Anglia over the following months raises the question: how much safety was compromised and what level of risk was the region subjected to? It was replaced in the next year by an improved version known as Yellow Sun Mk I, and it was not until mid-1961 that Bomber Command received what could be referred to as its first real H-bomb, code-named Yellow Sun Mk II.

In Moscow the Russians were also giving thought to how many well-aimed bombs would be required to annihilate the UK. In 1961 the then British ambassador Sir Frank Roberts was at a performance of the ballet when in an encounter with Khrushchev he was asked how many hydrogen bombs it would take to destroy the British nuclear arsenal. Hoping to minimise the scale of any attack the Soviets planned, Roberts said possibly six bombs. The Soviet leader indicated that his commanders estimated nine, but he thought that was optimistic, and so he had ordered his generals to allocate several scores of bombs for delivery on UK targets.

Conscious of the threat, from January 1962 Bomber Command placed one V-bomber per squadron, in total approximately fifteen aircraft, permanently on Quick Reaction Alert (QRA). That meant fifteen minutes' readiness to take-off fully armed with nuclear weapons. In addition four Valiants were also permanently at fifteen minutes' readiness at RAF Marham in Norfolk from RAF squadrons assigned to the Supreme Allied Commander Europe. This meant the V-force was being placed on an equal readiness footing to the Thor force, 24/7 and 365 days a year. A total of sixty-nine nuclear weapon systems was therefore always at the very highest point of readiness on Eastern England bases – fifty-four Thor missiles (allowing for up to six undergoing maintenance at any one time) and fifteen V-bombers. In the words of Air Marshal Sir Kenneth Cross, C-in-C of Bomber Command, the introduction of QRA changed the relationship between his command and the American Strategic Air Command from 'one of co-operation to one of integration'. It would 'reinforce the morale of the operating crews and staffs throughout the Command'. Britain was the third-ranked nuclear power in the world in 1962, able to target as many nuclear weapons on the USSR as the Russians could target on the USA.

For the V-bomber squadrons, Quick Reaction Alert meant ratcheting-up their alert status. Those crews on QRA ate and slept in quarters close to their aircraft. By the time of the Cuban missile crisis in October 1962, according to a former senior Bomber Command officer, Air Vice-Marshal Stewart Menaul, in his book *Countdown, Britain's Strategic Nuclear Forces*, the Thor force and V-bomber force together were capable of delivering a nuclear holocaust of 230 megatons on 230 targets. His assessment was that most of these nuclear weapons 'would have reached their assigned targets if orders had been given to attack'. Of course, this horrific outcome represented only a proportion of the nuclear bombardment which would have been delivered from UK bases. It takes no account of the nuclear punch which would have been launched by the USAF from its East Anglian Tactical Fighter Wings based at Lakenheath, Bentwaters and Wethersfield. These three units were equipped with F100 Super Sabres, each capable of carrying 1.1 megaton nuclear weapons. The integrated target policy included many targets that would have had to be hit in the first strike if there could be certainty of finishing the war quickly and limiting damage done to the UK and Western Europe.

The British system of QRA was different from the Americans'. They used a system of air-refuelled airborne alert. A proportion of their nuclear-armed bombers were in the air maintaining a vigil around the clock. However, V-bombers could not carry a second crew, as the Americans did, so long hours airborne, kept aloft by regular refuelling, was impractical for the RAF. Trials at RAF Waddington aimed at maintaining a credible airborne deterrent by changing over aircraft every six hours also proved impossible to sustain. The only solution for the V-force was the QRA concept. It was improved upon with the introduction of on-line tele-talk communications direct from the Bomber Command controller at HQ in High Wycombe to the crews, and by modification of aircraft to allow simultaneous four-engine starts. This reduced the time from the order to 'scramble' and being airborne to four minutes, the anticipated minimum warning time. In times of tension, as during the Cuban crisis, the whole V-force could be airborne within this timescale.

From August 1962 a revised joint RAF/USAF strike plan was introduced. It allocated to the RAF sixteen cities chosen as centres of administration and control; forty-four 'offensive capability' targets like airfields, ten 'defensive capability' targets like air defence control centres, and twenty-eight intermediate-range missile sites.

Individual Thor launch crews were responsible for checking that their missile was correctly targeted using an allocated target code, but they had absolutely no knowledge of what or where the target was. All that the Thor launch controllers knew was the sequence of numbers which had to be fed into the missile's guidance system to steer it onto the selected target in Soviet territory. The only people who were aware of exactly what targets the sixty Thors were programmed to hit were the senior officers at Bomber Command Headquarters and at the headquarters of Strategic Air Command in the States.

Each missile had two alternative targets allocated to it, and the crew had to be able to change a target setting in five minutes. A third 'target of opportunity' was available to be entered if the order was given, but this took longer to feed into the guidance system. The missile was aimed using two short-range electro-theodolites mounted inside the missile shelter when the rocket was horizontal. When it was erect, aiming was maintained through the long-range electro-theodolite housed in a small brick building some 400 feet from the launch pad.

Ernie Coppard, who was a launch-control officer at Catfoss, recalls:

> Target changes came to us as a series of numbers. The LCO on duty was required to check these numbers on a console while they were being changed by a technician, altering the position of a series of potentiometers in the guidance area. Targets were never given as placenames, and I never came across an LCO who showed the slightest interest in looking at charts to try to find out what targets might lie in the remit of our missiles. Better not to know!

Les Pettman was a missile servicing chief based at Bardney. He says:

> Targets were changed frequently and the targeting was checked on a daily basis. The target came in the form of a fifteen-digit sequence of numbers in a sealed envelope. We never had any idea where the missile was destined. Frankly we really did not want to know.

Sqn Ldr Ken Hayes, CO of 77 (SM) Squadron at Feltwell, remembers
that the targets

> *came down from on high. We didn't know what the targets were.*
> *They came in the form of a whole lot of numbers and there was a*
> *rather complicated procedure of sitting in the electric equipment*
> *trailer and inserting what were called new VGs, or velocities to be*
> *gained. The whole process was not as easy as it sounds.*

Bill Young, CO of No. 82 (SM) Squadron at Shepherd's Grove,
Suffolk, put down his recollections in 2000.

> *The crews never knew what or where the targets were (nor did*
> *the atomic warhead, unlike today's 'smart' missiles). They knew the*
> *'keel' and pad pointed roughly east – that the missile had a roll*
> *programme after lift-off, setting its path only somewhere within 15*
> *degrees of the original alignment, and that mysterious figures (VGs)*
> *were fed into the system that would tell the missile when to cut out*
> *the engine – leaving the warhead in 'free-fall' after its controlled*
> *trajectory through space.*

Gp Capt Kenneth Pugh AFC was in command of all the missile
launch sites in the Driffield complex. No one on the headquarters
base, or any of the other launch pads in the wing, knew the targets
their Thors were destined for. 'It was not politically a good idea we
should know', he says. There was an ongoing process of surveying the exact positions of the launch pads at regular intervals to
ensure the co-ordinates remained accurate.

Sqn Ldr Frank Leatherdale, CO at RAF North Pickenham in
Norfolk, remembered that there were several strange psychological
feelings working in a Thor squadron.

> *Not least of these was not knowing your target. During the war I*
> *had been used to being well briefed on precisely what our target was*
> *and why we were attacking it; but with missiles all you knew was a*
> *series of digits which had to be fed into the inertial guidance system*
> *very accurately and which had to be checked and rechecked several*
> *times a day. The checking was always done by the on-coming and*
> *off-going flight commanders together at every shift change, and was*

also done by other specialist personnel at other times in between. Another odd feeling we had was that we were working all the time to perfect our technique, but if ever we had to launch this deterrent weapon we knew we would have failed in our primary duty. Of course, being responsible for the safety of three nuclear warheads and all the expensive technical equipment was a continual mental burden. But I was not alone, for while I held ultimate responsibility I had very good support from my flight commanders, and they in turn were supported by their men. If ever the words 'a team effort' meant anything, they certainly did in a Thor squadron. Our watchword was continual vigilance and strict adherence to the check lists and manuals at all times.

Kenneth Moll was a captain in the US Air Force stationed at Caistor in Lincolnshire between January 1959 and March 1961, one of the launch sites of the Hemswell complex. He recalls that, as far as he was aware, Thor missile targets were determined by the Joint Strategic Planning Staff at Offutt Air Force Base in Omaha. This was a unit with representatives not only of the USAF, but also of the RAF and other NATO countries. The unit was commanded by General Thomas Power, commander of the Strategic Air Command. The targeting plan was known as the Strategic Integrated Operational Plan, or SIOP in the abbreviations loved by the American military. It detailed targets for strategic bombers, of the US and UK Air Forces, Thor missiles and later intercontinental and Naval Polaris missiles. Moll said:

Thor targets were not interchangeable on a whim. There were extremely strict controls on targeting, as there were on launch procedures. Thor targets were preset into the guidance system. Thors may have had several preselected target options, I can't recall, but the American authentication officer had no knowledge of what target was set into any particular missile.

He went on:

In my view Thor was a substantial deterrent because of its powerful nuke, its proximity to the USSR, and its invulnerability. Thor flight

time was 15 minutes – too quick for most Russians in a target region
to even flee to an air raid shelter. In comparison Strategic Air
Command bombers would take many hours to reach their targets.
In the early 1960s there were no anti-ballistic-missile capabilities
whatsoever. To defend against the Thor would have been as futile as
London defences against the V2. Thors were not to be ignored.

Quick Reaction Alert was part of a war readiness plan which, if there was a threat of attack, meant the next stage was for the nuclear-armed V-bombers to be ordered to widely scattered dispersal airfields. The idea was to make sure that the whole of the V-force could not be knocked out like sitting ducks by a pre-emptive strike. The next stage after dispersal in ratcheting-up the alert stance would be a decision to launch the deterrent. The crews of the V-bombers would be authorised to take off. The commander of Bomber Command then had two options. The V-force could fly direct to its targets if the executive order to launch a nuclear strike had been issued, or it could fly to pre-arranged go/no-go positions and await further instructions. If no instruction was given, the crews knew they should return to the UK.

This procedure guaranteed, as far as it was possible to do so, the element of political control. But the Thor force could not operate in the same way. Once launched, a ballistic missile could not be recalled, which is why some critics regarded Thor first and foremost as a 'first-strike' system. Government considered the only acceptable policy was only ever to use nuclear weapons in retaliation, or at least if there was evidence of an incoming hostile missile. Command and control was a major concern of Government and of the Chiefs of Staff. Discussions as to how the necessary controls could be exercised, given that warning times were becoming shorter and shorter, took up much time in Whitehall. In the early 1960s Bomber Command's Alert and Readiness Plan spelt out delegated powers in certain circumstances for the Commander-in-Chief of Bomber Command. He was, for instance, permitted to order an Alert Three on his own discretion. This authorised the maximum number of aircraft to be loaded with nuclear weapons and prepared for immediate take-off. Authority to escalate to the next stage, dispersal of the V-force, was not to happen without political authority. Only *in extremis*, if the C-in-C believed it necessary to avoid the destruction of the force on the ground by an enemy strike, could he order the force into the air, but then only under the procedure that required a further executive order for crews to proceed past the go/no-go point.

Despite these quite explicit arrangements, it was covertly acknowledged that circumstances could arise under which the C-in-C might have to assume responsibility for launching an attack – a military rather than a political decision. Such a decision would only be taken if it was impossible to get political authority because of a surprise Soviet attack which disrupted communications or wiped out the ability of the Government to exercise control. Macmillan stressed, however, that this was a last resort to be actioned only when it had been confirmed that nuclear weapons had struck in the UK. It was as a result of these considerations that in the early 1960s Macmillan agreed to the building of an alternative seat of government outside London. Variously codenamed Turnstile, Stockwell and Burlington, it was built deep underground beneath some fifty-four acres of Cotswold countryside near Corsham. Turnstile was destined to be the seat of government in the period following a nuclear attack. From this bunker authorisation for nuclear retaliation would come. The secret government HQ was planned to accommodate, in pretty Spartan conditions, some hundreds of key service and civilian staff. For very obvious reasons, Turnstile remained highly classified. If its location had become known to Soviet intelligence it would clearly have been a prime target. London as the centre of government obviously could not be concealed. Turnstile had to remain highly secret if the UK Government was to survive a nuclear conflict. Even planners in the various ministries, including the Ministry of Defence, who were making decisions about Turnstile, did not know its location. Most aspects of government which could not be exercised by the War Cabinet and nucleus of the Government at Turnstile would be devolved to regional seats of government, or 'citadels', of which, in the early sixties, there were twelve across the UK at places like Catterick, York, Nottingham, Cambridge and Dover Castle. The staff allocated to the RSGs included civil servants from a range of ministries, public information units including the BBC, the police and fire services, civil and defence control. Government in a rare public statement about the centres said the purpose of RSGs was not to protect the occupants but to enable succour and relief to be brought to the public after a nuclear attack and to marshal services and supplies essential for survival. If ever these centres had had to be manned, whether they would have accommodated their full complement of officials is questionable. Given the appalling circumstances of all-out nuclear conflict, how many of the civil servants and officials selected to run them would have abandoned their wives, families and children to face the awful consequences while they sheltered in deep bunkers? Regional commissioners would have full powers of the Crown and of Government in their own region, since there was no certainty that Central Government could rely on being able to give anything more than broad policy directions, and possibly not even that. There was another highly secret plan, codenamed Operation Candid, that dealt with the protection and evacuation of the Queen. For the general public the proof that nuclear war was a near-certainty would come when the BBC radio broadcasts fell silent and an hour later began retransmitting, renamed the Wartime Broadcasting Service (WTBS), from an emergency bunker in the Worcestershire countryside.

The Government's War Book laid out the steps to be taken under various scenarios. Early on in the Cold War the British Government visualised that there would be six months' warning of an impending war, a period during which international tensions would rise and planning could be put in place. One handbook published during the Cold War outlined the kind of contingency plans that would be put into effect:

Bans upon unauthorised assemblies will be enforced ... sandbags will go up around government buildings, while trains and lorries disperse their archives. The Territorial Army will be mobilised. Crash courses on civil defence will be organised for civil servants. Farmers will be advised which crops to quickly harvest. Command posts for use in civil emergencies will be manned. In the grounds of country houses prefabs will appear to serve as first-aid dressing stations. St Johns and the WRVS will be much in evidence as they set up emergency centres. Local authorities will post a list of do's and don'ts to each householder. Reassuring policemen and wardens with dosimeters on their chests will try to call at every house to back up the media's instructions on how to make fall-out shelters ...'

One is prompted to say, 'Pull the other one.' Was anyone really taken in by such optimistic propaganda? The Cuban crisis proved that events could move much more quickly; far too fast for civil defence measures to be activated; too fast for any realistic evacuation of large centres of population. So while the military went to the highest state of readiness in the whole of the Cold War over the threat in October 1962, none of the other carefully devised War Book plans were activated.

Government distributed 'protect and survive' leaflets to the civilian population, but it is hard to credit that Ministers and senior civil servants really believed that the advice they were giving would prove practical in the circumstances of a devastating nuclear attack. Official estimates believed a nuclear war would last only between two and seven days – the destructive phase. This would be followed by a survival phase during which both sides would be unable to continue fighting. Taking an optimistic view, this would lead into a reconstruction phase, though how long this would take and how effective it would be in enabling the recovery of the country after a savage nuclear holocaust could only be guessed at.

The success of contingency planning depended heavily on timely warning of a hostile attack. As weaponry was developed and improved on both sides of the Iron Curtain, the potential warning time steadily diminished. Before the introduction of the American ballistic missile early-warning system in 1963 the only means of detecting incoming missiles that Britain could rely upon was the giant radio-telescope at Jodrell Bank. Arrangements were made by the Ministry of Defence for the telescope to be realigned at an hour's notice to pick up Soviet missiles at a range of a thousand nautical miles. However, this was hardly a guaranteed warning system. Jodrell Bank had been built for scientific research. There were real concerns that the instrument might confuse missiles with atmospheric phenomena. So Jodrell Bank, it was conceded, could not necessarily identify an attack with any absolute certainty. This was the situation that had to be contended with during the Cuban crisis, and it highlighted the need for Britain's Thor force and V-bombers to be at the highest peak of alert. Warning might have been as minimal as an unheralded 'bolt from the blue'.

In 1963 the whole picture changed when Fylingdales, the ballistic missile early-warning station (BMEWS) in Yorkshire, was declared operational. Estimates of the warning that Fylingdales could give varied between twenty-eight minutes and four minutes. The shorter warning was likely to indicate an attack launched solely against the UK, in which case the radar would pick them up on a low trajectory, providing only minimal reaction time. The American BMEWS system had taken a long time to complete. It consisted of three long-range radar stations based in Alaska, Greenland and Britain. The UK would have preferred the third station to have been based in Lincolnshire or East Anglia, since this would have provided a swifter warning to Bomber Command forces stationed largely in those East Anglian counties. But it proved difficult to find a suitable site, which was why Fylingdales, in a government-owned national park, was chosen. Three radars were located at Fylingdales in the distinctive white radar domes: two scanned the horizon to look for hostile missiles; the third was a tracking radar to forecast the likely area of impact.

CHAPTER 12

A Heartbeat from Armageddon

B y 1962 the Soviet Union faced overwhelming force ranged against it. Perhaps it was not surprising Khrushchev should seek to redress the balance. From 1957 to 1961, he had repeatedly threatened the West with nuclear annihilation. He insisted that Soviet missiles were so much better and more effective than those of the United States. He could, he said, destroy any US or European city at will. He boasted to Mao, the Chinese leader: 'Now we have the transcontinental missile, we hold America by the throat. They thought America was beyond reach. But that is not true.' The only flaw in Khrushchev's boasting was that he had less nuclear capability than he was trying to convince his adversaries he had. In fact at the time of the Cuban crisis the American advantage in strategic weaponry was about seventeen to one.

In the late 1950s, when Eisenhower was convinced America faced a growing missile gap, Khrushchev was keenly aware that the United States had deployed missiles to the UK – the RAF's Thor IRBMs – and to Italy and Turkey in the form of Jupiter IRBMs. These missiles threatened the USSR from positions, from the Kremlin's point of view, uncomfortably close to home. Those in Turkey were less than a hundred miles from the Soviet border. Ironically, the stimulus for American deployment had, in part, been the missile bluff Khrushchev had indulged in. Now he reasoned that America too should learn 'just what it feels like to have enemy missiles pointing at you'. In deciding to base missiles in Cuba, under a highly secretive operation known in Moscow as 'Operation Anadyr', he declared, 'We'd be doing nothing more than giving them a little of their own medicine.' Khrushchev has gone on record as saying that the problem of how to defend Cuba 'was constantly on his mind'. In his memoirs he said that to lose Cuba would have been a terrible blow to Marxism–Leninism and would gravely diminish the USSR's stature around the world. 'We had to establish a tangible and effective deterrent to American interference in the Caribbean.' Cuba, he thought, was the ideal location for IRBMs. The Jupiters in Turkey and Italy and the Thors in Eastern England not only suggested a means of protecting Cuba, they also provided in Khrushchev's view a moral and even a legal justification. Not only would it be easy to strike at every major United States city with missiles based there. It would give the Soviets the ability to threaten America's unprotected back door. The US ballistic missile early-warning system faced north, the direction from which, over the horizon, intercontinental missiles would come. The US had no radar screen to warn of missiles fired from sites to the south, for example in the Caribbean. Such a move would at least double the number of Soviet missiles capable of reaching US soil. In a typically colourful phrase Khrushchev declared, 'We are going to throw a hedgehog into Uncle Sam's pants!' It was a hedgehog with some powerful prickles. The CIA estimated the Russians had at least thirty-two SS-4 nuclear missiles; launch sites for twenty-four SS-5s, which were at sea *en route* to Cuba, and twenty-four surface-to-air missiles ready to fire (one of which shot down an American U2 spy-plane on 26 October, killing the pilot). In fact the CIA had under-estimated Soviet resources. Russia also had on Cuba ninety-six non-nuclear anti-aircraft missiles, forty-two Beagle bombers, capable of carrying nuclear bombs, MiG fighter-interceptors and some 42,000 Red Army soldiers – in manpower alone four times the strength the CIA believed.

It was a remarkable logistical exercise for the Soviets to pull off in total secrecy. In fact, it was the largest amphibious operation the

Soviet Union had ever mounted, and the Americans seemed hardly to notice until the first U2 over-flights spotted the missile emplacements on 15 October 1962.

The Soviet missiles were capable of reaching almost all the main centres of population in the entire United States, and even parts of South America. The medium-range weapons could reach and destroy Washington, the Panama Canal, Cape Canaveral and Mexico City. The intermediate-range ones could hit most major cities from Lima in Peru to Hudson Bay in Canada. When the crisis broke, the Soviet Union had at least 158 strategic and tactical nuclear weapons on Cuba, forty-two of which could have reached some part of the United States of America.

Early on in the crisis Kennedy, questioning why Khrushchev had decided to place nuclear missiles in Cuba, told his national security adviser McGeorge Bundy, 'It's a goddam mystery to me . . . it is just as if we suddenly began to put a major number of missiles in Turkey. Now that'd be goddam dangerous, I would think.'

'Well we did', said Bundy.

'We did it in England, too', added Alexis Johnson, the Deputy Under-Secretary of State. At times, the knowledge gap between Administration and military appeared frighteningly wide.

In the months leading up to the Cuban crisis the United Kingdom and the United States had a secret weapon that served them well. In the murky world of espionage, MI6 and the CIA had an ace in the form of a colonel in Soviet military intelligence. His name was Oleg Penkovsky. Recruited by the British Secret Intelligence Service, Penkovsky had been passing high-level information on Russian nuclear capability to Whitehall and Washington since April 1961. Penkovsky was motivated by his conviction that Khrushchev's threats of nuclear war were real, and that his reckless unpredictability could well spark a nuclear conflict. So alarmed was he over Khrushchev's motives, in private he referred to Khrushchev as 'the atomic Hitler'. The material he sent to his handlers included technical information that suggested Soviet rocketry was far less advanced than the Russians were claiming. Penkovsky supplied literally hundreds of photographs and technical specifications of top-secret Soviet manuals, and even plans of

Soviet missile-site construction, which enabled the British and Americans to work out in detail the size of the threat represented by the Cuban launch sites, once the covert work on Cuba had been confirmed by aerial reconnaissance. His information included the range of Soviet missiles, their potential destructive power and how long it took to bring them to an operational state. These details helped the Americans to identify the types of missiles and warheads being installed on Cuba. Penkovsky's information was critical to Kennedy's approach as the crisis unfolded.

The first Macmillan knew officially of the threat in Cuba was on 21 October, when President Kennedy personally told the British Ambassador, Sir David Ormsby-Gore, of the Russians' clandestine deployment. However, there is evidence that senior British intelligence officials, who were visiting Washington, may have been briefed at least a day earlier, in which case the British Government would have learnt the broad facts some hours before the first exchange between President and Prime Minister.

Coincidentally, when the news broke, Bomber Command was in the midst of one of its regular command-wide alert and readiness exercises. Air Vice-Marshal Stewart Menaul, a senior Air Staff officer at HQ Bomber Command in 1962, writing in 1980, said that by 20 October the situation had deteriorated so seriously and rapidly that Bomber Command's Commander-in-Chief, Air Marshal Sir Kenneth Cross, was in continuous communication with the Air Ministry and with US Strategic Air Command headquarters at Omaha in Nebraska. It is certainly possible that the closeness of communications between Strategic Air Command and the RAF might have kept Bomber Command informed of events in advance of official communications between the White House and Downing Street. On the evening of 22 October, Kennedy, in a fifteen-minute televised speech to the nation, announced to the American public the evidence that the Russians were installing missiles on Cuba, and revealed that an immediate naval blockade, or as the diplomatic language termed it, 'quarantine', was to be set up around the island. As the President began his speech American forces across the world were placed on high alert, and the Strategic Air Command was ordered from DEFCON (Defence Condition) 5 to DEFCON 3, just two stages below actual war. Fifty-four SAC bombers took off, each carrying four H-bombs, to boost the twelve armed aircraft on twenty-four-hour patrol that America routinely sustained during the Cold War. As one aircraft landed on completion of its fully armed patrol another immediately took its place in the air. At the same time 136 Atlas and Titan intercontinental missiles were prepared for firing. SAC's move to such a high alert stance would have been signalled direct to Bomber Command. In his speech Kennedy told the American public that he had ordered the Pentagon to make all preparations necessary for military action. Defence Secretary Robert McNamara in a confidential report had listed the requirements: 250,000 men, 2,000 air sorties against various targets in Cuba, and 90,000 Marines and airborne troops for an invasion force. Troops were rapidly moving in to the south-eastern part of the United States, equipped and prepared. One estimate of American casualties if an invasion was ordered was over 25,000.

Air Marshal Sir Kenneth Cross's recollections seem to run counter to Menaul's account. Sir Kenneth is said to have tried to contact both the Air Ministry and Strategic Air Command during the early stages of the crisis, but without much success, so he was forced to act on his own initiative. It is not easy, so long after the event, to establish the exact sequence as events developed. A senior officer in Bomber Command headquarters during the crisis period recalls that they were fully aware of the state of Strategic Air Command's airborne alert, and of the move by the Americans to DEFCON 3. Sir Kenneth Cross and General Thomas Power, the commander of Strategic Air Command, were personal friends, and in the normal course of day-to-day events they were in contact on a regular basis. However, there are no actual records of what contacts may have been made, or what conversations may have taken place between them, as the crisis developed. It has been suggested in some records that from the point when Strategic Air Command raised its alert status the contact between the two commanders was less frequent, even non-existent. If that is true, it would certainly have put in jeopardy the dual authorisation procedure for the Thor missiles in the UK.

Macmillan, Sir Alec Douglas-Home, who was Foreign Secretary, and the Chief of the Defence Staff Lord Louis Mountbatten, were shown the first U2 photographs of the missiles in Cuba on the afternoon of 22 October, by the American Ambassador to the UK, David Bruce. Macmillan's immediate reaction was, 'Now the Americans will realise what we in England have lived through for the past many years.' He noted in his diary that night: 'This is the first day of the world crisis.'

In East Anglia, as the world crisis developed, eighty-five police from seven forces across the East of England guarded the V-bomber base at Honington in Suffolk as 300 'ban the bomb' demonstrators marched on the base. It was another CND protest that I witnessed as a member of the local press. Thirty-eight demonstrators were arrested, and two special courts sat until almost ten o'clock that night dealing with them. But from no one was there confirmation that Honington, in common with other front-line V-bomber bases in the region, was on high alert.

In Washington the climate of deep concern, even fear, of where the situation was heading was encapsulated by Kennedy offering Ormsby-Gore, the British Ambassador and his family, who were personal friends, places in the Presidential nuclear shelter deep beneath the Appalachian Mountains. The prevailing mood was of real foreboding.

The mood at three American airbases in East Anglia was similarly sombre. Several hours before Kennedy addressed the American people – well before any member of the public in Britain knew of the threat – the F100 Super Sabre squadrons at Lakenheath, Bentwaters and Wethersfield had been placed on covert alert, and armed with 1.1 megaton nuclear weapons. Since the RAF and Strategic Air Command were operating under integrated strike plans, there was a direct operational link between these American bases and the RAF Thor squadrons. The co-ordinated plan, described in a previous chapter, called in some instances for dual targeting. The Super Sabres were to deliver the first strike on certain nominated targets, to be followed literally within a minute by a Thor missile providing a follow-up blow. The concept was to guarantee annihilation of a target and maximise the chances of each and every target being knocked out before it could respond. It has been said that one Lakenheath pilot had the unenviable task of making his bomb run shortly after a Thor had struck, and in the knowledge that following him, within a further minute, a second Thor was due on the target. The fact that the Thor squadrons were permanently on a war-readiness footing, fifteen minutes or less to firing, and operating under dual-key arrangements between the RAF and USAF, meant that such a co-ordinated plan would not have been difficult to implement.

As the crisis developed and deepened, the US squadrons based in East Anglia were moved to an even higher state of alert. At its most critical, pilots were in their cockpits, ground power units attached ready to fire up engines, and the covers were taken off the loaded weapons. For some units the number of targets allocated and the number of aircraft at readiness was increased. Elsewhere in Britain, American B-47 bombers were loaded with nuclear weapons and prepared for take-off. At Holy Loch in Scotland, three American submarines, equipped with Polaris nuclear missiles, slipped quietly out to sea accompanied by their tender ship.

A proportion of Britain's V-force was, as always, at quick reaction alert, ready for take-off within fifteen minutes, if the order was given. But some RAF V-bomber squadrons based at Marham in Norfolk operated under a different command structure. They were assigned to the Supreme Allied Commander Europe (SACEUR). Some of these aircraft too were on fifteen minutes' readiness, meaning that the aircraft were fully fuelled, loaded with nuclear weapons with all switches set to rapid start on all four engines. It was normal for the aircraft to be locked and the pilot to carry the key on a string round his neck. Pilot and crew were not allowed to leave the dispersal area, and they slept fully clothed on camp beds. Crews were regularly exercised in rapid take-offs, and the V-force prided itself on being able to get airborne within the anticipated maximum four minutes' warning time.

On 22 October, as a DEFCON 3 alert was being ordered for the Strategic Air Command, the North Atlantic Council was briefed on the Soviet missile sites in Cuba. That same evening General Lauris Norstad, the Supreme Allied Commander in Europe, had a long-standing dinner engagement in London with Macmillan. The Prime Minister impressed on Norstad that overt provocative action in Europe, which a full NATO mobilisation alert would represent, could be counter-productive, indeed would exacerbate the situation. In his diary entry that night Macmillan wrote: 'I told Norstad that we would not, repeat not, agree to a NATO alert at this stage. Norstad agreed with this and said he thought NATO powers would take the same view. I said that mobilisation had sometimes caused war.' Macmillan had been deeply impressed by events that led up to the First World War, and was determined to avoid anything which might promote an unstoppable sequence of events leading to war.

Following this meeting Norstad sent a communication to Kennedy saying the Prime Minister favoured 'a strong but deliberative approach'. The official NATO stance he ordered was to move to an increased degree of vigilance without full mobilisation. Norstad's directive to his subordinate commanders ended with the following caution: 'No measures will be taken which could be considered provocative or which might disclose operational plans. Actions should be taken without public notice if possible.' However, not all Norstad's commanders followed his orders to the letter. General Truman Landon, the Commander of United States Air Forces Europe (CINCUSAFE), while not imposing a formal DEFCON 3 state of readiness, did allow some of the features of such an alert to be implemented. He independently ordered a discrete increase in the overall capability of his forces to be effected in a gradual and unobtrusive way. Significantly, this included an increase in the number of nuclear-armed aircraft on quick reaction alert and their loading with high-yield thermonuclear weapons in place of less destructive, lower-yield nuclear bombs. Some of these changes to the alert stance involved RAF V-bombers under NATO command at bases in East Anglia, notably Marham.

It was also 22 October when Penkovsky's luck ran out. The KGB had been closely monitoring Penkovsky's activities for some time in order to learn about other potential agents and the operation of the West's espionage networks. However, after Kennedy had announced publicly the discovery of missiles in Cuba, the Soviet counter-intelligence authorities needed to know rapidly what information Penkovsky had passed to the UK and America. He was arrested in Moscow and interrogated intensely. Subsequently, when the Cuban crisis had been resolved, he was tried for treason and espionage and executed early in 1963.

It was at the suggestion of Ormsby-Gore, at a meeting in the White House on 23 October, that the decision was made to draw the quarantine line around Cuba at 500 miles, rather than the 800 previously agreed. The British Ambassador argued that this would give the Soviet ships approaching from Europe, loaded with further missiles and equipment, more time to react, and provide Khrushchev with greater opportunity to decide his next move. Ormsby-Gore also pressed Kennedy to take Macmillan's advice and immediately release the incriminating U2 photographs of the missile emplacements to the media – a shrewd move which had a powerful impact on world opinion. At this stage twenty-five Russian ships were *en route*, fourteen of which were believed to be carrying missiles. By Wednesday 24 October, fifty-six American warships were moving south to establish the blockade. That same morning Kennedy gave the order to start the countdown for 'Operation Scabbard', the codename given to preparations for the invasion of Cuba. The plan was to build up to a force of 90,000 Marines and airborne troops with the aim of hitting Cuba on 30 October.

In Britain Macmillan's instinct was still to counsel restraint. Having lived through two world wars, he felt strongly that overt mobilisation could itself be a cause of war. He was worried that any over-reaction by the Americans in the Caribbean would pro-voke the Soviets to move against Berlin, which would immediately escalate the threat of a third world war. In his diary, though he never said this in public, Macmillan noted that the American blockade in the Caribbean was illegal, and it might be hard for neutral and even friendly countries to accept it. In the States a rather different view was being expressed. General Curtis Le May, the notoriously pugnacious Chief of Staff of the Air Force, advocated bombing the Cuban bases immediately, without warning. He was clear about what to do: 'The Russian bear has always been eager to stick his paw in Latin-American waters. Now we've got him in a trap, let's take his leg off right up to his testicles. On second thoughts, let's take off his testicles too!'

'How will the Russians respond?' asked Kennedy. 'They'll do nothing', Le May confidently replied. 'Are you trying to tell me that they'll let us bomb their missiles and do nothing?' Kennedy asked. 'If they don't do anything in Cuba, then they'll certainly do something in Berlin.' After this exchange, back in the Oval Office, Kennedy remarked to a member of his staff, 'Can you imagine Le May saying a thing like that?' He added pointedly that the generals had one thing going for them: 'If we listen to them and do what they want us to do, none of us will be alive later to tell them that they were wrong.' The White House position was that history would neither accept nor forget a USA-initiated 'Pearl Harbor' attack on a small nation without warning.

The mood in Washington and other parts of the USA was getting close to fear. In the White House envelopes were distributed to key personnel with the message, 'To be opened in emergency'. These contained the passes and instructions on where to report to be taken by helicopter to deep shelters in the case of a warning of nuclear attack. A poll taken in the States on 23 October showed one in five Americans believed the blockade would result in a third world war. Earlier in the year the Kennedy administration had issued to the US public a guide to the facts of thermonuclear war, advising people on the steps they could take to provide limited protection for themselves. Twenty-five million copies of the 46-page booklet had been printed, and the Department of Defense had allocated nearly $700 million for civil defence, including the construction of fall-out shelters and stockpiling of emergency food supplies and medical equipment. Evidence of this came to light in 2006 when a long-forgotten storage room under New York's Brooklyn Bridge was opened to reveal 350,000 packs of civil defence emergency rations, medical kits and water-drums, dated 1962.

On Wednesday 24 October, with surveillance indicating further rapid progress in building the missile launch sites and Soviet ships, escorted by submarines, continuing to head for the blockade line, the Strategic Air Command's state of readiness was raised even higher, from DEFCON 3 to DEFCON 2 – the highest alert state that could be ordered short of all-out war. Air Force General Thomas Power took the decision apparently with no communication with the politicians. He sent the message in clear uncoded form, aware that the Soviet authorities would pick it up and understand its implications instantly. The change in status moved the alert in the

USA up a gear, which meant an eighth of Strategic Air Command's bombers based in the States would at any one time be airborne with nuclear weapons aboard, awaiting instructions to proceed beyond their 'hold' lines.

In East Anglia, a reporter from the local newspaper *Eastern Daily Press*, aware of the growing concern being expressed on the other side of the Atlantic, contacted a spokesman at the giant American base at Sculthorpe in Norfolk, only to be told: 'We have no comment to make.' In 1962 Sculthorpe was the biggest nuclear bomber base in Europe, with some 10,000 personnel stationed there. Third Air Force Headquarters at Ruislip were no more forthcoming: 'We are not in a position to comment beyond what the President himself has said.'

On the Thor bases in England USAF personnel reacted with unconcealed tension to the DEFCON 2 order. Their RAF launch-crew colleagues remained covertly in a high state of readiness under the cover of a Bomber Command exercise, but the RAF's alert status remained several notches below that of the Americans. One launch-control officer recalls learning of the American DEFCON 2 order when he went into the American authentication officer's cabin to find the status board showing the alert state altered and the American officers in a high state of excitement. Another recalls being shocked to see American colleagues armed and openly on edge, constantly on the phone to their Operations Centre. Former Sqn Ldr Syd Hudson, who was CO of 98 (SM) Squadron at Driffield, remembers American officers rushing into the officers' mess armed with revolvers, wound up about the order from Strategic Air Command. The consequences of the two national partners, both of whom would have been essential to the launch of an armed missile, operating under different alert states must have raised potential issues for both air forces.

Mr Jo Grimond, the Liberal leader, while sympathising with the anxieties being expressed in America, issued a statement saying that the Americans maintained bases round Russia that were open to similar objections that America was expressing about Soviet missiles in Cuba. 'If America retaliates,' he said, 'Russian retaliation on American bases threatening the Soviet Union could be justified on the same grounds.' He clearly had in mind the Thor bases here in England. It illustrated the heated debate and growing concerns among politicians on this side of the Atlantic.

On 25/26 October further photo-reconnaissance of the ongoing work on the Cuban missile sites was obtained. The Americans sent in some risky low-level over-flights to capture absolute confirmation of what was taking place. What the photo-reconnaissance could not detect, however, were the ominous orders that the Soviet forces on Cuba had received from Moscow. Files of the Central Committee of the Communist Party, released in the 1990s, clearly indicated that as Cuba was too far from the Soviet Union to be reinforced in the event of an American invasion, the Russians would have relied upon tactical nuclear weapons. Unknown to the Americans, Russian troops on Cuba were equipped with such tactical nuclear armaments in the form of short-range Luna rockets carrying 2-kiloton nuclear charges. Khrushchev had given General Issa Pliyev, his military commander on Cuba, authorisation to use these nuclear weapons without prior approval from Moscow.

Russian commanders have since confirmed these weapons would have been used to repel any American invasion force that attempted a landing on Cuba. Furthermore, four Soviet submarines, sent to make their home base in Cuba, were equipped with nuclear-tipped torpedoes, and their captains had been given the same authority to use them without reference to Moscow.

Alarm bells were ringing ominously at the United Nations. U Thant, then UN Acting Secretary-General, commented, 'Mankind's very existence is in the balance.'

At the British Ministry of Defence a spokesman went on record as saying that no British military moves were being made as a consequence of the Cuban situation – a less-than-accurate statement that would have sounded far from the whole truth to those RAF men waiting tensely on quick reaction alert beside their nuclear-armed V-bombers, or sat in launch-control caravans on the Thor sites with their missiles minutes from a possible launch.

In Britain, on Friday 26 October, Air Marshal Sir Kenneth Cross, on his own authority, extended the Bomber Command alert and readiness exercise to enable him to maximise the command's capabilities in the event of war. It was convenient that the 'smoke-screen' of an ongoing command exercise avoided any overt order being made which might have alarmed the British public. According to Air Vice-Marshal Menaul, in the early hours of the next morning Cross went into the operations room to discuss the exercise with senior staff and to hear the latest news from America, in particular President Kennedy's statements on the gravity of the situation. The C-in-C decided to further increase the readiness of the force, under cover of the training exercise. These instructions were given over the broadcast telephone system from the operations centre, and within seconds the orders had been flashed to all stations. As a result, on all V-bomber airfields, mostly in East Anglia and Lincolnshire, there was a requirement to double, in most cases to six, the number of fully armed aircraft at quick reaction alert, on fifteen minutes readiness or less. At one base, RAF Waddington, the number was trebled to nine. At this point all British nuclear forces were on full alert, able to be launched in less than fifteen minutes against some 230 targets. The late Air Vice-Marshal Jack Furner recalled a strange air of unreality in the Bomber Command Headquarters bunker. He described it as an extremely tense time; the unreality of the situation being emphasised by the fact that in the outside world life in Britain went on as normal, neither the public nor the media seeming to be aware of the implications for them of the growing threat imposed by events thousands of miles away.

On 27 October, which became known as 'Black Saturday', came further proof of Soviet resolve. At around 10 a.m. a U2 spy-plane, being flown by Major Rudolf Anderson, the pilot who had gleaned the original evidence of missile pads on Cuba, was shot down by a Soviet surface-to-air missile. Anderson was killed. The order to fire had been given by Lieutenant-General Stepan Grechko, commander of Soviet air defences in Cuba, without referring to Moscow. In political circles in America and Britain there was alarm that the Russians were deliberately escalating the crisis. In Moscow Khrushchev panicked. Reports reaching the Kremlin suggested Kennedy was about to announce an invasion of Cuba. What made the events of 27 October, the most critical day of the crisis, even more dangerous, was the fact that many thousands of miles from Cuba another American U2 had inadvertently entered Siberian air space. When Soviet MiGs scrambled to intercept, the

Americans ordered nuclear-armed fighters from a base in Alaska to meet them. In a situation where military tension was on edge on both sides, the possibility of war starting by accident through misjudgement or misunderstanding was terrifyingly plausible. There is evidence to show that to keep a hugely increased fleet of nuclear-armed B-52s continuously airborne some may have flown with weapons whose circuitry had not been certified as safe. Elsewhere, in the scramble to get the maximum of new silo-based intercontinental ballistic missiles ready, some Minuteman crews bypassed safety procedures and virtually 'hot-wired' their weapons, risking an unauthorised launch.

As a result of the uncertainty in the Kremlin, the Russians were sending out conflicting signals. The same morning a private letter from Khrushchev to Kennedy reached the President's desk. In his letter the Soviet leader called the blockade 'piracy'. 'You are threatening us with war', his letter declared. He then offered a deal: the Soviet Union would state that its ships bound for Cuba 'will not carry any kind of armaments' if the United States would declare that it did not intend to invade Cuba. Khrushchev's letter ended: 'These thoughts are dictated by a sincere desire to relieve the situation, to remove the threat of war.' But no sooner had the President read Khrushchev's message than an Associated Press communication came over the wires noting that a further statement had been issued in Moscow, reporting that Khrushchev had told the President he would withdraw offensive missiles from Cuba only if the US withdrew its rockets from Turkey. The Kremlin had issued a new, more aggressive letter – this time publicly – which significantly changed the terms of the deal. Khrushchev's second letter said:

> ... you have surrounded the Soviet Union with military bases, surrounded our allies with military bases, literally disposed military bases around our country, and stationed your rocket armaments there. You are worried by Cuba, you say that it worries you because it is a distance of ninety miles by sea from the American coast. However, Turkey is next to us, literally at our elbow.

This new twist in diplomatic exchanges raised the level of concern in capitals across the world.

In London Sir Thomas Pike, the Chief of the Air Staff, was called by Macmillan to Admiralty House. Admiralty House was being used as Macmillan's office while renovation work was being carried out at 10 Downing Street. Macmillan and Pike discussed what measures might be taken to alert United Kingdom forces, and again the Prime Minister expressed his strong wish that overt preparations should be avoided. He stressed he did not want Bomber Command openly alerted, although it should be ready to take 'appropriate steps' if it became necessary. Immediately following this meeting Pike contacted Air Marshal Sir Kenneth Cross to tell him that 'he should be on the alert and that his key personnel should be available on station'. At 1 p.m. the fiction that Bomber Command's readiness alert was all down to a routine readiness exercise was over. Cross officially ordered Bomber Command – the V-force and the Thor ballistic missiles – to Alert Condition 3. Whether this was a step beyond the Prime Minister's instructions, when he said overt preparations should be avoided, is a matter of conjecture. However, F.W. Mottershead, deputy secretary of the Ministry of Defence at the time, was quoted in 1993 as saying, 'Nothing in my recollections, nor in that available in the Ministry of Defence, is at variance with the indication that higher authority was not sought for the measures taken by Bomber Command.' At 3.47 p.m. on Sunday 28 October, Cross tightened the screw still further. He issued additional instructions, increasing the number of aircraft armed with nuclear weapons, ready to go and with crews on quick reaction alert. These enhanced Alert 3 conditions remained in force until 5 November.

Normally, this level of readiness would have been accompanied by an order to disperse the V-force to their dispersal airfields. Each main V-bomber base had six dispersal airfields, widely scattered across the UK, which they could use to minimise the whole force being wiped out in a first-strike attack. However, the Prime Minister's explicit instructions to do nothing that overtly drew attention to the fact that Bomber Command had been put on such a high state of readiness prevented Sir Kenneth Cross, much to his chagrin, from taking that precautionary measure.

The late Gp Capt Roy Boast, who was CO of the Hemswell complex of Thor launch bases, writing in 1998 recalled:

I was advised by the Air Officer Commanding Group early on the Saturday morning that we were on standby for the real thing but that, apart from the early recovery of the missile on maintenance, manning and procedures would be as for any other day with all the sites continuously manned. I did not inform my wing or squadron commanders of the AOC's message, but anyone abreast of the news would recognise for himself the full implications. The next thirty hours seemed most unreal, doing all the normal things with my wife and daughter (my son was away at school and had the best chance of us all of survival). Perhaps the worst thing was to realise that the station and dispersed sites would be hit and destroyed shortly after we had fired our own missiles, or before if the Russians chose to make a pre-emptive strike.

At another Thor base a launch-control officer, looking back to 1962, reflected: 'We did very little but we thought a lot.'

At a hastily convened meeting at 2.30 p.m. on Black Saturday, the UK Navy and Army Chiefs of Staff were briefed, and the Joint Chiefs agreed that 'at the moment no further action is needed other than that of alerting key personnel'. However, it was also agreed that Bomber Command aircraft should be dispersed in the event of 'positive indications that the US propose to operate against the Cuban mainland'. The Chiefs were also told that any US invasion would not take place until 29 October, a day earlier than Kennedy had first anticipated. The British Government, the Chiefs were told, would be informed before any definitive action was taken, but this might be in the form of information rather than consultation. The Chiefs of Staff put on record their views, including the various alert measures that would have to be taken, for discussion in Cabinet, if it was decided to hold a Cabinet meeting at short notice. Historians believe that at this point Macmillan was just hours away from calling a crucial Cabinet meeting that would have taken the fateful steps towards war and authorised, for the first time, the dispersal of his Government to its secret bunkers – Turnstile, and the various regional centres of government across the country.

Meanwhile, exceptional activity was taking place at Marham in West Norfolk. Three Valiant squadrons based there operated, as already explained, under the command of the Supreme Allied

Commander Europe, and therefore fell under orders issued by the American General Landon. In the event of war they were to be armed with American Mark 5 nuclear weapons, which were exclusively under the control of USAF personnel. US law insisted that loading of American nuclear weapons had to be supervised by American officers. Normally this represented no particular problem. Whenever an aircraft was armed and on fifteen minutes QRA it was held in a secure compound and only released after the Americans had received an authenticated order on their own dedicated channels. However, during the missile crisis orders came through to arm all available aircraft. It was impossible with the relatively small number of Americans on the base to maintain the strict system of custody-and-control protocol demanded by US law. So the control of the weapons had to be handed over to the RAF base commander. A total of twenty-four Valiant bombers, each armed with two American nuclear weapons, were put under the effective control of Bomber Command, although legally the agreement between the US and UK governments meant they had to be regarded as still under the ownership of the USA.

It was during Black Saturday, 26 October, that the flash-point occurred that came close to triggering a third world war. The US Navy in the Caribbean was unaware that Soviet Foxtrot submarines, operating off Cuba, were carrying nuclear-tipped torpedoes. On the most dangerous day of the confrontation, only hours after the shooting down of the U2, a drama unfolded that is now recognised as the single incident in the whole Cuban crisis that came nearest to igniting Armageddon. Some of these events only became known in 2002, when a meeting was held in Cuba to mark the fortieth anniversary of the crisis. It was attended by former military men and politicians from America and Russia who had been closely involved in the crisis as it unfolded.

The Soviet submarines were heading towards Cuba to spear-head the development of a Soviet naval base at Mariel Bay. Under orders from the Pentagon, US ships were carrying out systematic efforts to track the submarines as part of the naval blockade. The US ships were under orders not to attack the submarines directly, but to induce them to surface and identify themselves. Messages outlining US Navy intentions were transmitted to Moscow. US authorities ordered their ships to drop practice depth-charges whenever a naval task force identified a Soviet submarine, to signal it to surface. This involved considerable risk. The Soviet crews were exhausted by weeks submerged, and hearing depth-charges being dropped they were alarmed they were under attack. It is now known, from information published in Moscow in 2002, that senior officers in several of the submarines considered firing their nuclear torpedoes, each of which carried a nuclear yield equivalent to the bomb dropped on Hiroshima. Aboard one submarine, B-130, which the US destroyers had cornered, Captain Nikolai Shumkov ordered preparation of the nuclear-tipped torpedo. The weapons security officer warned him the torpedo could not be armed without permission from headquarters. Tension on board was running at such a level that the security officer reportedly fainted under the strain. Shumkov told his crew he had no intention of using the torpedo because if he did so all of them would perish.

Even more dangerous was what happened aboard the submarine B-59. In a remarkable account published forty years later, the communications intelligence officer, Vadim Orlov, recalled the tense situation that developed when the vessel came under attack from American depth-charges. A totally exhausted Captain Valentin Savitsky, unable to establish communications with Moscow, and believing a war had already started, ordered the nuclear-tipped torpedo to be made ready for firing. Three officers on board – Savitsky, the political officer Ivan Semonovitch Maslennikov and Commander Vasili Arkhipov – had authority to launch the torpedo, providing they all agreed. A furious argument broke out between them, in which only one, Arkhipov, was against making the attack. Eventually he persuaded Savitsky to surface the submarine and await orders from Moscow. At the conference in 2002, marking the fortieth anniversary of the missile crisis, the former American Defense Secretary, Robert McNamara, acknowledged that Arkhipov, by his persuasive arguments, had almost certainly saved the world from a nuclear war.

In the White House the American attitude to the fifteen Jupiter missiles in Turkey was under anxious review. It was recognised they could pose a dangerous trigger to war. The Secretary of Defense, MacNamara, was concerned that Turkey might fire the missiles, without presidential orders and in defiance of the dual agreement, if she was attacked by the Russians in retaliation for an attack on Cuba. He repeatedly suggested that the United States should defuse the rockets before any military action against Cuba. He was concerned that Turkish officers, if they seized the warheads, might retaliate independently against the Soviet Union. Significantly, there were no similar concerns expressed during White House discussions about the far greater nuclear strike power represented by the sixty British-based Thors.

However, there is evidence that Macmillan was pondering using the Thor missiles as a bargaining chip in the dangerous game of chess that was being played out. At the height of the crisis Macmillan conceived the idea of immobilising the Thors in return for the Russians' dismantling their missiles in Cuba. He thought it might help Khrushchev to save face. He was also almost certainly aware that the decision to phase Thor out over a period of months had already been taken. The suggestion of using Thor as a bargaining chip was passed to Kennedy, but the President was worried about the impact of dismantling too many weapons on the West's deterrence capability, and the implications it would have for NATO.

However, backed into a corner by Khrushchev's conflicting private and public proposals, Kennedy decided to take the initiative by replying publicly to the Soviet leader's initial open letter, and not Khrushchev's more defiant private message. In his response Kennedy said he would agree to a 'permanent solution to the Cuban problem along the lines suggested in your letter of October 26th if 1. You would agree to remove these weapons systems from Cuba ... 2. We, on our part, would agree ... (a) to remove promptly the quarantine measures now in effect and (b) to give assurances against invasion of Cuba.' Simultaneously, through his brother Robert Kennedy, the US Attorney General, the Russian Ambassador Anatoli Dobrynin was told, face to face, that the missiles in Turkey would be removed in accordance with Khrushchev's wishes. The President wanted them out, too, but later and not in public.

On 28 October the US Foreign Intercept Service began picking up an extraordinary message broadcast by Radio Moscow. It came in the form of an open letter from Khrushchev to Kennedy. The

Soviets were clearly alarmed by the speed events were moving. 'The Soviet government', the message read, 'has ordered the dismantling of bases which you regard as offensive and their crating and return to the Soviet Union ... I regard with respect and trust the statement you have made in your message ... that there would be no attack or invasion against Cuba.' The breakthrough had come at almost the last minute. It was less than forty-eight hours before the American invasion was due to start. There had been no public mention or public statement from either Washington or Moscow of the American climb-down over the Jupiter missiles.

No wonder the American networks were calling it an 'American victory'. A few days later Kennedy invited the Joint Chiefs of Staff to the Oval Office to thank them for their role. General Curtis Le May told him there was no reason for thanks. 'We lost! We ought to just go in there today and knock 'em off.'

Time magazine a short time later reported a conversation in West Germany between the Soviet Ambassador and a high-ranking German diplomat. 'As objective diplomats we must admit', said the Russian, 'that American rocket bases in Britain, Italy and Turkey are legally and morally the same as the ones we are dismantling in Cuba, mustn't we?' 'I admit no such thing', the West German said. 'It seems to me they are entirely different.' But were they? Did Khrushchev, despite his bluster and his hostility, have a point? The threat posed to Washington from Cuba was no different from the threat posed to Moscow from the Thors in England. It is arguable that had Khrushchev carried out the deployment of missiles to Cuba publicly and openly, claiming they were there at the behest of Cuba's sovereign government, in the same way that Jupiters were in Turkey and Italy, and Thors in the UK, he might well have claimed moral and legal justification. But he chose to carry out Operation Anadyr in secret and then direct his diplomats in the United States and the UN to deny the truth.

The Americans eased the naval blockade on 2 November, following Khrushchev's decision to remove all his IL-28 bombers stationed in Cuba. That day Kennedy went before the American public again on television. He confirmed that aerial reconnaissance showed the missile bases being dismantled and the missiles and associated equipment being crated.

A Foreign Office observer commenting on the dramatic events of that October summed up what had happened as 'the world's most public snub to the world's most publicised prima donna'. The world thought Kennedy had forced the USSR into a humiliating climb-down. It was much later that it became clear Khrushchev had not walked away empty handed. The Jupiter missiles threatening his country had been quietly removed from Turkey, and within a year the Thor missiles in the UK would be gone, too.

There was one further incident that still has historians and commentators arguing over exactly what took place and for what motive. The British and American handlers of Col. Penkovsky made elaborate arrangements, under the codename Distant, to ensure that the West received a direct warning if a Soviet nuclear attack was imminent. Penkovsky was supplied with two telephone numbers in Moscow. If he received information that the Soviets were about to launch an attack he was told to ring one of the numbers and blow into the mouthpiece three times, wait a minute and then repeat the procedure. He was told not to speak on the phone, but if at all possible to leave further detailed information in a secret 'dead-drop' location. The telephone signal on its own would be considered a warning message of the highest importance; meaning either that the Soviet Union had decided to attack, or that an attack would take place if the West failed to take specific action. It was impressed on Penkovsky that the UK and US authorities would act on his warning immediately. On 2 November, eleven days after he had been arrested (although at that time neither MI6 nor the CIA knew of his arrest) the Distant emergency procedure was activated. The two calls were received one minute apart and someone blew three times into the mouthpiece each time. When a CIA agent went to see if anything had been left at the dead-drop point, KGB officers were there, and the CIA agent was arrested and interrogated. Clearly Penkovsky had told the KGB how to activate the Distant warning. But had he told the KGB exactly what the signal meant? By activating it, the KGB had given the West the signal that a nuclear attack was imminent. Why? Was it that Penkovsky, knowing he would be put on trial and executed, let the KGB unknowingly, in effect, press the nuclear button in the hope that a military response from the UK and US would be his final revenge on the Soviet system he hated? Or was it that the KGB, aware that the period of highest crisis had passed, used the procedure to find out more about Penkovsky's contacts? It could have been disastrous, but his SIS controller in the British Embassy in Moscow, even before it was known that the CIA agent had been arrested, was convinced the signal could not be genuine, and fortunately made his advice known swiftly to Whitehall and Washington. Three days later, on 5 November, Bomber Command's unprecedented Alert 3 was withdrawn, and the Thor force and V-force reverted to their normal round-the-clock vigilance. The Americans maintained their Cuba blockade and their peak alert until 20 November, when it became clear that Khrushchev had kept his side of the bargain.

Why did British nuclear deterrent forces stand down so much earlier? One theory that has been advanced links the decision to the activation of Penkovsky's Distant code after SIS's master spy had been arrested. Was it that Penkovsky, in a last throw, tricked the KGB to using the Distant warning in the hope that it would trigger a nuclear attack on Russia? Remember, he had agreed to work for the West because he was convinced the Kremlin was hell-bent on prosecuting a third world war. Could it be that the British Government lowered the alert status early, deliberately to reduce tension in Moscow?

CHAPTER 13

Minutes to Launch

On the Thor bases Bomber Command's Alert 3 triggered an urgent drive, all the way down the East of England, to ensure that the maximum number of missiles were brought to within fifteen minutes of launch or less. It was normal practice to keep 65% of the Thor force on permanent fifteen-minute standby, a unique war-ready stance in time of Cold War peace. The October 1962 alert resulted, in a fairly short time, in fifty-nine of the sixty missiles being brought to a peak of readiness, each armed with a nuclear warhead.

For the crews there was no escaping the gravity of the situation. They knew what the public did not know; that events in the Caribbean were considerably closer to home than media reporting, or indeed any Government comment, indicated. There is evidence from former Thor crews, who recall the tense hours and days at the height of the crisis, that on some bases the missiles were ordered to a more advanced stage than fifteen minutes to launch. This was what was referred to as a T-8 or Phase 2 hold, meaning that the countdown had been initiated and taken through the first two stages of the five-stage process. At this point, before the missile was loaded with liquid oxygen and RP-1 fuel, it could be held in the erect position, eight minutes from firing. Squadron Operational Records (ORBs) provide no confirmation, but launch crews recollect that their missiles were ordered to the erect position, which would

145

indicate a shorter-than-usual readiness state, a substantial step nearer to firing.

As Senior Technician Ian Killick recalls, at Feltwell the missiles were taken to T-8, and the training missile on the base was recovered from its training role, armed with a nuclear warhead and brought to a wartime state of readiness. 'This was the most frightening three days of my life', he remembers. 'It was an experience that will hopefully never be repeated. We were convinced that this would be it. However, it was not easy to think logically knowing that sixty missiles across all the launch sites were minutes from lift-off.'

He recalls that on the five sites of the Feltwell strategic missile wing 'we got fourteen of our fifteen missiles into this phase of readiness without any major problems, and kept them in this state for nearly three days.'

Gp Capt Kenneth Pugh AFC was the officer commanding the Driffield Thor complex, where all fifteen missiles spread across five launch sites in East Yorkshire were brought to within seven or eight minutes of firing. 'We were no more vulnerable on the missile bases than anyone else in the country', he said. Looking back, he did not recall any apprehension on the station or in his own feelings. 'Had it been forced upon us there is no question the missiles would have been fired, but we were quite convinced the deterrent was going to work; perhaps we had an infantile simplicity about our beliefs.'

Gp Capt Pugh's son Peter was thirteen at the time. He went on to pursue a career in the RAF, reaching the rank of wing commander. All the Thor missiles being erected and brought to the end of Phase Two of the countdown procedure and held there for days on end was unprecedented, and made a deep impression on him as a boy. Despite his father's recollection of little in the way of apprehension, Peter Pugh says he was well aware of his father's tension at the time. 'The threat was very real and I carry the memories of that time to this day', he says. 'As a thirteen-year-old it made a strong impression on me.' He remembers that he and his mother were briefed to pack small kit, and told they might have to go to RAF Patrington, where there was a deep radar bunker. Driffield, everyone knew, was bound to be a primary target. Peter

Pugh says that when the alert was over there was a palpable sense of relief.

Brian Jennings was a member of a launch crew based at North Pickenham in Norfolk. He remembers being called to a briefing by his squadron commander, Sqn Ldr R. Henderson, at which crews were given an outline of what was happening. Launch crews were doubled up and shifts extended.

> I was allocated to Pad Thirteen (lucky for some!). After carrying out initial checks on our missile like all other pads, we carried out a countdown to the end of Phase Two, which in effect checked out all the basic systems. We retracted the shelter in which the missile was housed and erected it on its launch mount and securely locked it in place. It was now vertical to a height of nearly 70 ft. At this point the countdown was put on hold. The only thing left to do was to fuel the missile, which would take approximately three minutes, and from then on she would be ready to launch. After carrying out a further check on the targeting of the missile, we retired to the electrical equipment trailer, from where we could monitor the power systems and carry out retargeting if called upon to do so. At frequent intervals further checks were undertaken on pneumatic and hydraulic systems housed in various trailers around the launch pad. I seem to remember a calmness about it all, with everyone doing their duties in an air of normality which belied the seriousness of our situation.

Mr Jennings recalls being ordered to stand by for an important message broadcast through crew headsets. 'It was a rallying call that put people in the picture and made clear the grave position we were in. The tension was racking up and everyone was worried about what might happen, and the effect on our families if war broke out and we had to fire the rockets in anger.' Brian recalls later returning to the house he had been allocated in the village of North Pickenham to find his children playing with new toys that had been bought for them for Christmas. He asked his wife how they had got them. 'Barbara replied, "I gave the toys to them because if we are all not going to be here much longer they might as well enjoy Christmas now."'

He adds: 'At that time disaster was literally only a few minutes away. The British contribution during that time should be remembered. It was equally important as the American effort.'

Sqn Ldr Bill Young, in command of the Shepherd's Grove launch pads in Suffolk, remembers missiles being taken to a stage even further into the launch process:

> *At the time of the Cuban crisis all the missiles were brought to readiness, and to save launch time, kept fuelled and 'on hold' at the end of Phase Three. This meant that the individual missile hangars were rolled back, the missile target system 'captured', the launcher retracted, and liquid oxygen allowed to boil off through a safety valve. All sixty readiness lights in the 'ops' room at Bomber Command shone a brilliant green. It would have taken only another two or three minutes to complete Phases Four and Five, ending with ignition and lift-off. It was a very tense and nerve-racking time indeed. As the squadrons were only too aware, the missile sites stretching from Suffolk to Yorkshire would be prime and essential targets in any 'shooting war'.*

Sqn Ldr Colin Burch was in command of No. 218 (SM) Squadron based at Harrington in Northamptonshire, one of the group of Thor launch sites in the North Luffenham complex. Later he was appointed training officer for the whole North Luffenham group. During the missile crisis he was in the North Luffenham control room standing by for instructions from Bomber Command Headquarters. He recalls that no crews were allowed to leave the base. The RAF were aware that their American colleagues were on a higher state of alert and always seemed a step ahead, which was the cause of plenty of friendly banter. 'We felt the Americans were on edge, very tense. They seemed to have a mania for security.'

The missiles could not be held in a high state of readiness, minutes from firing, indefinitely. Liquid oxygen in the missiles boiled off at an alarming rate. Bill Young, from his perspective commanding the Shepherd's Grove launch pads, recalls: 'In spite of the British Oxygen Company's valiant effort, the UK was slowly running out of this vital fuel and the tankers to transport it. "Green" readiness lights turned to "red" as squadrons reserved enough fuel for a final launch if needed.'

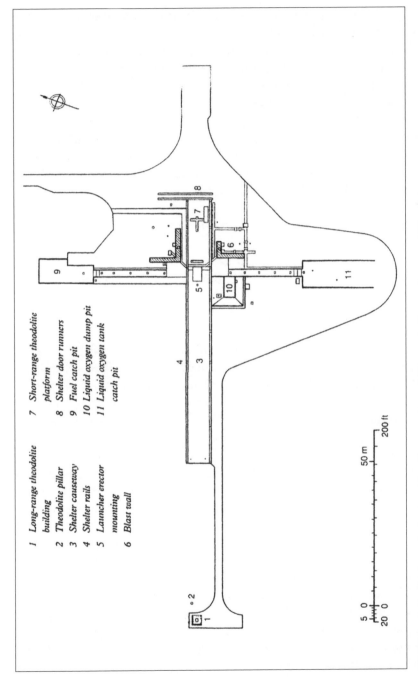

1 Long-range theodolite
  building
2 Theodolite pillar
3 Shelter causeway
4 Shelter rails
5 Launcher erector
  mounting
6 Blast wall

7 Short-range theodolite
  platform
8 Shelter door runners
9 Fuel catch pit
10 Liquid oxygen dump pit
11 Liquid oxygen tank
   catch pit

RAF North Luffenham, Leicestershire. Survey plan of Thor missile emplacement No. 3.

It was a strange parallel world in which the RAF crews at missile launch pads and V-bomber bases were at a state of unparalleled Cold War alert, poised to engage in an unthinkable nuclear exchange, while the public were blissfully unaware of the tension mounting around them. This unreal situation has been confirmed by no less a witness than Marshal of the Royal Air Force Sir Michael Beetham. In October 1962, Sir Michael was a group captain (operations) serving in the control room at Bomber Command Headquarters. Speaking of that time at a RAF Historical Society seminar in 2001, he recalled being at Command headquarters with the C-in-C, Air Marshal Sir Kenneth 'Bing' Cross.

> As soon as the missile crisis began to develop we got the message from Government, from Macmillan, that no overt action was to be taken. So anything that we did decide to do had to be done quietly. We couldn't, for instance, use the BBC to recall people from leave, as we would have liked to have done. In fact, we were so successful that nothing ever seemed to appear in the press, despite the fact that we had generated the entire V-force to a very high state of readiness. We even put the crews in their cockpits at one stage, but basically they were held at fifteen minutes' notice. Ideally, once the bombs were on board, what we wanted to do was to move on to the next stage in our pre-planned alert procedure, which would have dispersed the V-force. We were forbidden to do this, however, so the aircraft had to stay at their main bases.

Speaking to me in 2007, Sir Michael told me that Macmillan was anxious to 'play the whole thing down'. While the American Strategic Air Command was on airborne alert with nuclear-armed aircraft in the air twenty-four hours a day awaiting the command to proceed to their targets, the RAF was not allowed to use any method of public recall to contact front-line crews who might be on leave or off-station. Crews had to be recalled by telephone. Similarly, all aircraft on training missions overseas had to be unobtrusively called back to the UK. Despite the restrictions imposed by the Prime Minister, all necessary V-bombers were generated on all main bases, fuelled, armed and with crews on quick readiness stand-by and briefed for their potential targets. 'We would have liked to have dispersed the V-force for its protection had the situation worsened, but Macmillan's insistence on no overt measures made that impossible', he said. Bomber Command Headquarters was in constant touch with the Ministry of Defence, and operations officers worked up to twenty hours a day while the crisis was on.

Had the Government permitted dispersal – considered by RAF chiefs as essential to protect the UK's V-fleet against a Soviet first-strike attack – the V-bombers would have been dispatched to some thirty airfields scattered across the UK. Each had operational readiness platforms specially built alongside the runway for this purpose. Most were well away from the main bomber bases in the East of England, although Coltishall in Norfolk, a former Battle of Britain fighter base, had facilities for two V-bombers. Another dispersal site was Stansted, now London's third civil airport. Others were in Scotland, Wales, Northern Ireland and the South-West.

Sir Michael said that, looking back, the Cuban crisis was a very traumatic experience for all those involved, both at station level and at Command Headquarters. 'Strangely enough, the rest of the nation seemed to be quite unaware that there was a crisis at all When we went for a meal or took a break outside, the sun was shining and the media were obsessed with some football match. It all seemed quite unreal.'

What also seems unreal, forty-five years on, is that the Government, knowing how close nuclear war might be, took no steps to protect the civilian population. The Home Office, the Ministry responsible for protecting the public, appears to have done nothing, simply hoping the crisis would go away. A former Civil Defence officer in Norwich, one of the major centres of population down-wind of a nuclear attack on the significant V-bomber and Thor bases, has confirmed that no measures were taken to provide any kind of civil defence for communities in East Anglia. The fact that the Government apparently decided not to activate the largely voluntary Civil Defence organisation is remarkable, given the investment that had been made in it. Across the country an army of some half-a-million volunteers had been recruited and trained. Perhaps this failure to take even the most basic steps to prepare the public, in the face of the fact that the military clearly contemplated a possible nuclear attack, was to avoid public panic. But had the worst happened, the UK population would have been left to fend for itself. It was a huge risk that the Prime Minister and the Government took.

Macmillan did not want to alarm the British public. In the event, his gamble succeeded. Had it not, the population would have been exposed to the terror of nuclear war with little or no pre-arranged help. It also appears no steps were put in hand to activate the Regional Government Headquarters of which there were twelve in secure bunkers across the country. The role of these regional centres of government had been planned to ensure that essential administration continued up to and after a nuclear attack. They accommodated civil servants from across Government, including the Home Office the Ministries of Health, Transport, Public Works, Labour and Agriculture, and the Treasury. All the armed services were planned to be represented, the Central Office of Information, the BBC, the courts and even the Post Office. The flaw in the planning, however, was that it was assumed there would be weeks of warning as international tension escalated. In the event of a sudden unpredicted attack, or as at the time of Cuba, swiftly moving events, there was literally no civil defence or contingency planning.

Keith Harris, who was a chief technician based at Feltwell, working on Pad One, says the Americans, who had custody of the warheads, got quite excited during the crisis period. 'The bomb compound was close to our site and there was a great deal of action taking warheads to satellite launch sites. We had no hang-up as regards firing if the Russians had fired first, but I am not too sure the Americans were as steady as one might hope.'

Sqn Ldr Ken Hayes was CO of No. 77 (SM) Squadron at Feltwell. His recollection, borne out by the records since unclassified, is that the Americans were ordered to a higher state of alert early in the crisis:

The American authentication officers were ordered to remain permanently in the launch-control trailer at all times [he said]. It was even impossible for them to take a loo break during their shift. We remained, as I recall, at Alert Five until late in the crisis, when

Bomber Command ordered Alert Condition Three. I got the book out and did all the things I was supposed to do, including issuing the RAF police with ammunition and recalling people from leave, and then reported to the Wing Commander Ops, only to be told that we were to take covert measures only. Basically that meant reversing some of the steps I had taken. One action I do recall was to recover one of my three missiles – the sixtieth Thor – from training use, get it ready for operational purposes, and get the Americans to put a nuclear warhead on it. My thoughts were that something really was going to happen. I phoned my wife, told her that she should be ready to get the kids and necessary supplies and be ready to get under the stairs if the worst was to happen.

Sqn Ldr Hayes said he would not have questioned launching a missile if he had been ordered to do so. He had considered and discussed with his crew a possible scenario where there was a total breakdown of communications and they might be left sitting there with missiles but no contact with higher authority. 'We came to the conclusion that if we had irrefutable evidence that the UK was under attack and we knew we had lost contact with Bomber Command, we would at least contemplate launching anyway.'

At Catfoss, one of the dispersed sites associated with the Driffield complex, Jack Gilchrist was a 23-year-old missile servicing chief:

Many other members of the crew were World War Two veterans and had seen it all before. We had of course trained for this eventuality and could ready the missile very quickly indeed, each launch crew being given an 'Exercise Respond' at least two or three times per shift cycle of nine days. When the real thing came it was a Respond alert without the exercise anomalies – all personnel went about their business without panic or fuss. We were well aware that the Soviets had similar missiles and aircraft targeted on us, and that in the event of hostilities we were likely to be eliminated quite early on unless we launched first. Very early on in the crisis we went into a double-shift routine (two crews covering twenty-four hours a day doing twelve-hour shifts) so that a backup crew was readily available without having to travel the nineteen or so miles from the main accommodation base at RAF Driffield. I personally went to work one day and did not return home until nearly a fortnight later.

As at other bases, Jack Gilchrist recalls each of the three Catfoss missiles being taken to Phase Two hold, armed, ready for fuelling, and eight minutes from firing. At this point the missile shelter was retracted and the missile locked in its raised position. In this state the inertial guidance system was aligned and held in alignment by the long-range electro-theodolite, known as the LRT. The capturing of the guidance-system gimbal mirror to retain alignment on the target was the responsibility of the missile service chief. A Thor missile could remain in this position for long periods. To any outside observer with minimal knowledge, the missiles standing vertical on their pads were clear evidence that they had been taken to the final stage of war-readiness. Those who lived in the vicinity can readily recall the unusual site of the missiles upright and held there for a considerable period. There was also the tell-tale absence of crews at their usual evening haunts in nearby rural pubs. At Feltwell it was the unusual lack of RAF customers at the West End pub in the village that signalled the high state of readiness on the base.

Joe Froggatt was a Thor electrical wireman on 102 (SM) Squadron based at RAF Full Sutton, one of the launch bases attached to the Driffield Wing. He writes:

How did we feel about possibly having to launch such a deadly weapon which could kill millions, and also perhaps be the target of reciprocal action? Speaking personally, I found life just went on. This was a time when we had done the theory about the power of nuclear weapons; we'd heard about Hiroshima and Nagasaki, but the media cover at the time was far less intense or immediate. We were within the 'institution' of the RAF, and I suppose I couldn't or didn't want to consider just what might happen. If anything was to happen it was beyond our control. I recall our CO's answer to the question, 'What should we do if or when we fire our missile?' The answer was, 'Take your things and just go home.'

Wg Cdr Stanley Baldock, who was awarded the MBE for his work on the Thor programme, was Wing Commander Operations at the headquarters of the Hemswell Wing. Because of his seniority, unlike the launch crews and the majority of the personnel on the

Thor force, he was aware that the order issued by Air Marshal Cross on so-called 'Black Saturday' was 'for real', and there was a distinct possibility that missiles would have to be fired in anger. He recalls:

I was told I had got to stand by ready to respond to the top-secret message we would receive. In truth I really believed nuclear conflict was about to happen. My wife was going off to school with the children. I went back to the house to see them off and then went upstairs and got on my knees and prayed, because I thought it was the end. I prayed to God he would step in and that this disaster would not come about.

Another chief technician concerned with the maintenance of Thor recalls the missiles being held at peak readiness for several days. 'We were the first target in any conflict, and everyone accepted that position, although it was obvious the public had no idea what was really going on. The missile system itself was very good and we all had confidence in it. The majority of Thor personnel were long-term servicemen who understood the commitment to the job.'

There is anecdotal evidence suggesting that on some launch sites, notably at Hemswell, and, as Sqn Ldr Bill Young has recorded, at Shepherd's Grove, missiles were taken to an even more advanced stage in the countdown procedure, to a point where they were held fully fuelled at the end of Phase Three, four minutes from firing. However, the CO of the Hemswell complex, the late Gp Capt Roy Boast, does not refer to this in his memories of the crisis, which he wrote down in 1998, but other former crew members recall missiles fuelled with LOX and the clouds of vapour, which were a clear indication of tanks fully laden with liquid oxygen.

Len Townend, a missile maintenance technician working in the Training Section at Feltwell, recalls that he was sent to the operations room at Feltwell which controlled all the launch pads across East Anglia in the Feltwell group.

We were on standby in case a technical problem arose at any of the sites and our expert help was needed. It was a traumatic experience, especially as my wife and family were in married quarters a few hundred yards from the building I was in, and like everyone there we knew if a conflict started we were all a prime target. Looking back I shudder with horror at what might have happened.

Les Pettman, who was a chief technician at Bardney, one of the satellite launch sites in the Hemswell complex, says that had a Russian missile been fired from Cuba at the United States, the RAF Thor crews knew they would face a situation where they would be ordered to fire some or all of their missiles:

If President Kennedy had reached across his desk for the red telephone and said America had been attacked, I have no doubt we would have been ordered to fire in anger. As far as we were concerned, Kennedy was the boss. The Americans had invested heavily in developing and installing the Thor missiles in the UK, and if he had given the order they would have been launched. If we had fired in anger we knew there would have been no 'out' for any of us. We probably would all have died in the process.

This, of course, raises the crucial and almost certainly never-to-be-answered question: Would the British Government have had a veto on Thor being fired from UK launch sites had a situation arisen where, despite British Government opposition, the Presidential order was to launch? All those personnel who worked on the Thor bases believe that if the chips were down the dual-key arrangement could easily have been over-ridden. It would not have been difficult to relieve the American officer of his key that armed the warhead – by force if necessary. The Americans were far outnumbered by their RAF colleagues. However, the operations of Bomber Command and Strategic Air Command were so intertwined at planning and control levels that it is difficult to imagine such a fundamental dispute arising under operational conditions. How the politicians would have viewed it is another matter. There is, however, evidence to suggest that as well as the UK/US co-ordinated plan, Bomber Command also had a national plan, in the event that circumstances arose where British nuclear forces had to go it alone to defend national interests. This was an unlikely scenario, but the nature of military planning was to plan for the unthinkable. How Thor, under dual-key protocols, would have fitted into that national plan, if indeed it ever did, has never been revealed. Perhaps to have done so would have gone too close to revealing whether Thor ultimately was there as a defence of Britain, or actually to defend America.

Meanwhile, on bases housing the V-bomber force in East Anglia and Lincolnshire, crews were ordered to fifteen minutes' readiness, a similar state of combat alert to the missile launch crews. Peter West was a flying officer, the air electronics officer in the crew of the CO of a Vulcan squadron at Coningsby in Lincolnshire. He recalls:

The Cuban missile crisis started for us with a call-out from our homes. All of us lived on station or very close nearby. Trained and ready to respond to any call-out, we assembled at Ops within a short time, where we were briefed by senior staff, changed into flying kit and bussed out to the waiting aircraft. We had been warned that we would have to remain at readiness state fifteen minutes indefinitely, which meant that we would sleep and eat beside our aircraft. This was the first time that all of us on the three squadrons at Coningsby had been called to such a high state of readiness together, and it was awesome to see all the aircraft 'bombed-up' with nuclear weapons. The bomb-doors of each aircraft were left open so that the bombs could be attached to the 'fish fryers'. The 'fish fryer' was an item of ground equipment which looked uncannily like the frying machines in fish-and-chip shops. The purpose of this gear was to keep the weapon primed and heated, an essential operation if they were loaded onto the aircraft ready to fly. I should emphasise that we never flew with live nuclear weapons on board. These were only loaded for quick reaction alert exercises, or at the time of a real crisis, and this was just such a time, indeed the only time it was believed to be necessary.

There was no tedium during our long wait. We were friends and there was plenty of banter, conversation and, when that faded, reading material. I can honestly say that I detected no sense of fear or foreboding. This was not bravado or misplaced courage, simply that we all had total confidence in the policy of deterrence which we had discussed often. It was our belief then, and it remains to this day, that provided we made it clear that we would not hesitate to retaliate in kind to any nuclear threat, these awful weapons would never have to be used. To illustrate the point, on the second day of standby another member of the crew and I were sitting together reading when he put down his newspaper, slowly rose from his seat, strolled over to the aircraft and, pulling a chinagraph pencil from his pocket, drew a large CND symbol on the side of the bomb. When he returned to his seat I asked him why on earth he had done this. His reply has remained with me over all the intervening years: 'If we have to drop this beast then those CND bastards were right.' We never did have to drop the beast: those CND bastards were wrong!

During their time at a high state of alert there were periods when crews were called to cockpit readiness. Peter West recalls that on these occasions there was

a not unnatural feeling of tension. We knew with certainty that should the policy of deterrence fail then not only would we almost certainly not survive (our chances of getting back in one piece were assessed at only 20%) but more importantly our wives and children would also be dead as the airfields were high-priority targets for Soviet attack.

At RAF Wittering, near Peterborough, alongside the A1 road, on that Saturday, 27 October, all available Victor aircraft and crews were at cockpit readiness. Each aircraft was loaded with a free-fall thermonuclear weapon, and the crews were in possession of their secret bags containing all necessary route and target information, and the vital authorisation codes should the order to proceed be delivered. Crews remained at cockpit readiness for several hours before the state of alert was marginally reduced.

Each V-bomber crew had a dedicated target throughout their tour of three years. The details of this were kept in Operational Headquarters in a room called 'The Vault', windowless, sealed and guarded by armed RAF police. The target material was kept in a special safe controlled by a dedicated ops officer. Each crew-member had his own target folder containing everything he needed to know. Command and control of the bombers was in the hands of the bomber controller at Bomber Command Headquarters. He was in radio contact with every crew-member. Nuclear release was a tightly controlled system. Once airborne, each aircraft headed for a go/no-go line on a predetermined longitude. To continue beyond that line, authorisation had to be received by Morse code or voice. This was a coded message, and three members of the crew had each to verify it independently of one another. If the aircraft reached the go/no-go line without receiving the message, they had to return to base. Of course, had the crisis descended into war, it could well have been the RAF V-bombers, and not the USAF, that would have been first on the scene. The V-bomber crews knew this. They also knew that their role was to deliver their weapons with little hope of returning home – indeed with little hope of having homes to return to. The crews were expected to endeavour to return home, though some considered their best hope of survival might be to conserve fuel by turning off two engines and pray they could reach British bases in the Mediterranean.

While Britain's deterrent forces were poised on an unprecedented level of war-readiness alert, there was, apart from the lack of any Civil Defence measures, another inexplicable gap in preparedness. The Royal Observer Corps, who from the late fifties had eschewed their original role of aircraft spotting and reporting for a new and vital task as the national nuclear warning and monitoring organisation, was never activated during the Cuban crisis. In the early sixties the ROC operated from some 873 scattered underground bunkers equipped to undertake bomb-burst, fall-out and radiation monitoring. At least ninety-five of these were in Norfolk and Suffolk; areas considered prime targets because of the extent of RAF and USAF bases and Thor launch pads. A further fifty-five were scattered across Lincolnshire, where many V-bomber bases were located. But there was no alert to call in ROC volunteers in October 1962. Had the crisis developed as rapidly into nuclear war as many in Bomber Command feared, this essential service that was routinely exercised would not have been ready.

Almost immediately after the Cuban crisis had passed, within ten days of the relaxation of the Bomber Command Alert 3, Air

Marshal Cross held a Commander-in-Chief's conference at North Luffenham. The post mortem on how the command had risen to the challenge was attended by all his group, station and squadron commanders. He particularly praised the performance of the Thor squadrons. 'The Cuban crisis really showed the value of this missile', he told his audience. 'Without visible change fifty-nine of the sixty missiles had been made serviceable and ready simply by use of the telephone.' As Sqn Ldr Colin Burch, one of those who was there, said: 'We came out with halos!' What criticisms 'Bing' Cross had were directed at the V-force, not the missile squadrons.

On the other side of the Iron Curtain similar preparations for war readiness against American and European bases were also ordered. Although there are no official records to indicate exactly what orders were issued, some former Soviet military officers recall that missile units were brought to 'Combat Mode' during the Cuban crisis for the only time in the Cold War. In his book *At the Abyss*, former Secretary to the US Air Force Thomas C. Reed records that the Russian R-7 and R-16 rockets were stored, like the Thors, horizontally and unfuelled until made ready for use. Both types carried 2.8 megaton thermonuclear warheads. Orders to fire were relayed over poor telephone lines direct from Moscow or by code over a shortwave radio link. When received they were authenticated against a code sealed inside an envelope and held by the senior commander, who had to acknowledge receipt of the order back to Moscow. However, there was no centrally controlled system to prevent a crew launching without official authorisation, other than Red Army discipline. Reed quotes a staff officer from Rocket Corps Headquarters who at the time of the Cuban crisis was driving between rocket units based in the Urals. He was disturbed to see tanker trucks filled with rocket fuel heading towards the launch sites. Deeply concerned, he went to the telegraph desk at a divisional command post and was shown instructions from Moscow to bring rocket forces to 'combat readiness'. In that alert stage the weapons were to be held with armed warheads, communications frequencies were changed and operational documents distributed. It was a situation that had never ever happened before in the Soviet Strategic Rocket Force. The officer recalled that the faces of his colleagues showed three feelings: shock, because the Rocket Force had never before been ordered to such an advanced combat mode; alarm; and determination.

Thomas Reed writes in his book:

In my conversations with senior Russian officers, most point to October 1962 as the time when reality dawned. That week of watching and waiting on full nuclear alert while Kennedy and Khrushchev faced each other down gave officers up and down the line in the East and West time to think about their families ... That week of forced reflection made Americans and Soviets realise that their families, their children, and millions of other innocents, would be consumed by the fires of hell if things went wrong. During those six days in October the possibility of nuclear war changed from a policy option to a dreaded disaster.

Undoubtedly the Cuban missile crisis resulted in compromise however it was spun from the American side at the time. It was a crucial turning-point in the Cold War from which each side concluded that neither should ever again run such risks. Britain was in the middle, relatively powerless to influence any outcome, yet hugely involved and with absolute certainty a potential battle-ground. If it had come to a nuclear exchange it was unavoidable that the UK and Europe would have been involved. The crisis convinced the world's leaders that their own nations' survival depended upon the survival of their adversary – the philosophy of MAD – mutually assured destruction. The West avoided destruction, but the price was duration, a lengthy Cold War that dragged on for decades longer. In retrospect, there is a bitter irony in Khrushchev's decision to keep secret his attempt to establish missile launch pads on Cuba, and even to allow his diplomats to lie about his intentions. Had Khrushchev been open in his policy it could have been much harder for the US President to contest it. After all, the United States had deployed Thor to the UK and Jupiter to Turkey and Italy, as the world knew. What Khrushchev was unable to get away with covertly, he might well have been able to persuade world opinion, in open argument, was simply a balancing of power; a repetition of what the USA had already set as a precedent and had asserted was both justified and legal. Castro and Khrushchev had concluded a formal agreement between two sovereign states in August 1962 for the deployment of missiles in Cuba, but the Russians had refused to make it public.

CHAPTER 14

Political Cover-up?

The record suggests that the senior politicians in London – the Prime Minister, the Foreign Secretary, and the Defence Minister – were not entirely aware of the dramatic increase in the alert stance of British nuclear forces during the crisis. The late Lord Solly Zuckerman, chief scientific adviser to the Ministry of Defence in 1962, has been quoted by the American author Scott Sagan in his book *The Limits of Safety* as saying that, although he was at the centre of things he did not recall the Prime Minister, the Secretary of State or the Chief of the Defence Staff being directly involved with the order to raise the state of alert of Bomber Command. 'To the best of my knowledge,' he recalled, 'the Ministry of Defence did not order him [Air Marshal Cross] to increase the readiness state of his force.'

Lord Healey (Denis Healey) who became Secretary of State for Defence in the Labour Government two years after the crisis, told me in 2007 that politicians were absolutely not aware that Bomber Command had ordered such a high state of readiness. 'One of the really striking things of that time was the quite exceptional and unnecessary secrecy in Britain. Bomber Command was able to prepare for a massive raid on the Soviet Union without even letting the Ministry of Defence know, let alone Parliament.' That was 'shocking, and absolutely disgraceful'. Nobody in the general public had the slightest idea of what was going on. Lord Healey commented that in the aftermath of the Cuban crisis it was clear that a Government that wanted to keep public support for its defence policy had to be honest about what it was doing.

During the crisis the Ministry of Defence explicitly told the British press that increased alert measures were not being taken. So the British public were ignorant that their nuclear forces had gone to the brink of war. Macmillan made no mention of the British military stance when he told the Commons on 31 October, 'The world has had a shock. We have been very near the edge.' The Macmillan Government had previous 'form' in keeping disturbing news out of the public eye. In 1957 the Prime Minister had taken steps to heavily censor the report into the fire at the Atomic Energy Authority's Windscale plant in Cumbria, caused almost certainly by ministerial pressure on scientists to meet the demands of producing Britain's first megaton bomb. Macmillan, desperate to prove to the Americans that the UK was a reliable partner with which to share nuclear secrets, ensured his government remained tight-lipped about the alarming extent of radioactive fallout from the accident at Britain's first reactor. The first really major accident of the nuclear age was the subject of a political cover-up not dissimilar to that which followed the placing of the UK's deterrent forces on close to a wartime footing during the Cuban crisis.

The first inkling that covert events had moved the UK closer to nuclear conflict than at any other time in the Cold War, far closer than most people ever appreciated, came in a front-page report in the *Daily Mail* on 18 February 1963, three-and-a-half months after the crisis had been resolved. Under the front-page headline, 'When Britain went to the Brink', the article by the *Mail*'s defence correspondent, Stevenson Pugh, said, 'The sixty Thor rockets and the V-bombers in this country were "all systems go" for attack during the Cuban crisis. Categorical denials were given at the time that any preparations were being made. Now I learn that for the first time the Thors were poised in anger with H-bomb warheads in place; the bombers also had bombs ready.'

The report said the alert had been surrounded by official secrecy and that Macmillan had been within hours of informing the nation of his decision to back Kennedy all the way, when Moscow radio announced Khrushchev's decision to back down. At that point, the report continued, Bomber Command had been on its hair-trigger alert for eight days.

The *Daily Mail* reported that Air Marshal Sir Kenneth Cross issued his first alert on 20 October. On that day, it said, he found that fifty-nine out of the sixty Thor rockets were serviceable. It was a Saturday, but a proportion of bomber crews and V-bombers were also on standby in a state of readiness at the end of the runway on each V-bomber base. On the Monday, the sixtieth Thor, which was 'out' of operational use for training, was ordered to war readiness. All bomber crews were stood by. Sir Kenneth then received a request from US Strategic Air Command for a statement on his readiness. The request came on his own H-war network from SAC HQ in Omaha. The report commented that there seemed to have been no similar communication on the political network in Whitehall, despite the fact that the Thors and V-bombers were supposed to be responsible for a vital proportion of SAC's first-wave targets.

Records now released, and the recollections of those who were concerned at the time, bear out the basic facts in the *Daily Mail*'s report, although the dates in the newspaper report conflict with defence records. However, when, a few days later, Opposition MPs questioned Macmillan on the report in the House of Commons, the Prime Minister denied that anything other than what would be considered 'normal' had taken place. Labour MPs asked him if he had given authority for alerting V-bomber crews and Thor rocket bases in preparation for nuclear war. Macmillan replied that the V-force and the Thor rockets in the UK were always at a very high state of readiness. He added that during the period of tension, though not on the date mentioned in the *Mail*'s report, 'Certain precautionary steps were taken, but more than this was not necessary.' One Labour MP, Mr Stephen Swingler, persisted, asking: 'Is the Prime Minister calling the *Daily Mail*'s defence correspondent a liar? Is he saying his detailed allegations are false, or is his answer about precautionary measures a formula for concealing the fact that the Government were preparing a national suicide pact at the time of the Cuban crisis?'

The Prime Minister replied, 'Naturally, if the deterrent is to play its role it has always to be kept at a high state of readiness. During the period of tension certain additional steps were taken, but they were of a kind which is merely intended and normal.'

Another Labour member, Mr K. Zilliacus, asked, 'Is the Prime Minister telling the House that he was prepared to enter a nuclear war, which would have destroyed the people of this country, in support of an act of aggression by the United States which had resorted to force in violation of the UN Charter?' Macmillan replied, 'The honourable gentleman is making a quite false deduction from what I said and what was done.'

Asked by a further Labour MP, Mr Tom Driberg, if he would say why categorical denials had been made that any precautions were being taken, the Prime Minister said that what was denied was that some abnormal action was taken. 'This was a normal procedure by a force which is kept at a much higher state of normal readiness than any other force.'

How far Macmillan was aware of the details of Bomber Command's alert procedures, and whether he even remembered details of the permanent readiness stance of the Thor missiles in the UK, is questionable. It was rare for ministers to take a close interest in major nuclear deterrent exercises, and therefore not surprising that they did not appreciate all the implications, or were necessarily aware, of the routine levels of readiness that Britain's nuclear forces maintained. Macmillan was clearly concerned that overt mobilisation could provide its own momentum to war. In America, it seems, the reverse was true. When the Strategic Air Command was ordered by its military commander to DEFCON 2, the order was broadcast openly, so that the Russians would inevitably pick it up and take a sober view of where events might be heading.

When one looks back from a perspective of some forty-five years, there is no doubt that the British public were kept in ignorance of what was being done in their name; that the very close integration of America's Strategic Air Command and Britain's Bomber Command inevitably drew UK deterrent forces into a greatly enhanced state of alert; and British politicians were largely kept out of the loop of what RAF commanders were doing.

The position was summed up afterwards by Air Marshal Cross when he commented that, during the crisis, from him downwards everything worked perfectly; from him upwards, he perceived nothing worked at all. It is hard, given the records and the recollections, not to come to the conclusion that at the very least, during the crucial days of the Cuban crisis, there was a disconnect between the military command in the UK and the higher levels of government that in theory directed them. The Chief of the Defence Staff, Earl Mountbatten, at a meeting of the Chiefs of Staff when the crisis was over, asked, 'What would we have done if the Russians had not pulled back? Do we know? We've got to work this one out.' But no one seemed to know the answer. Air Marshal Sir Kenneth Cross in his actions undoubtedly remained within his delegated responsibility, but it seems, with good reason, that he pushed the authority delegated to him to its limit.

Duncan Sandys, Minister of Defence, speaking in the House of Commons in February 1958 had given a categorical assurance that the 'joint-decision' agreement under which the Thor missiles operated included special arrangements for rapid consultation between the two governments. Any decision concerning them would be taken, and he emphasised this point to MPs, by both governments and *not* by military commanders. In the event, the increased state of readiness that the Thors and the rest of Bomber Command were ordered to was taken by an air marshal without reference to his political masters, let alone any consultation between the two governments.

Papers released at the National Archives in March 2006 show that in November 1962, after it was thought the Cuban crisis had been resolved, Downing Street was shocked to learn that its American allies had, in fact, been poised to launch a third world war without formal consultation with Britain. A report from Maj-Gen Sir Kenneth Strong, director of the Joint Intelligence Bureau, indicated how serious the situation had become in the full heat of the crisis. 'The Americans were prepared to go it alone, either without consulting their allies or irrespective of what their allies said, had the Russians reacted against any action in Cuba by moving against Berlin', the note to the Prime Minister said. 'General Strong thought the American Government was prepared for their action in Cuba to escalate into the nuclear. It seemed to him that the US administration was over-confident that they had pinpointed the position of all the main sites of intercontinental missiles in the

Soviet Union, and they hoped they would be able to take these out with a pre-emptive attack by their bombers.'

In the Soviet Union Khrushchev rationalised the position as he saw it: 'It was a great victory for us', he wrote. 'We had been able to extract from Kennedy a promise that neither America nor any of her allies would invade Cuba.' He went on to state that the aim of America was to destroy Cuba, while his aim was to preserve Cuba. Who won? 'It cost us nothing more than the round-trip expenses for transporting the rockets to Cuba and back.' It was Castro who had the last laugh. He and his regime were still flourishing four-and-a-half decades later.

Macmillan and Home, the Foreign Secretary, were horrified that their allies, who they thought had consulted them from the early stages of the crisis, seemed to have been only paying lip service to joint discussion. They worried that America was dangerously gung-ho about fighting a nuclear war, which the United States assumed it could win. The unspoken factor, of course, was that it would have taken American aircraft operating from UK bases to achieve what the Americans might have had in mind. And at that time there was close integration between RAF Bomber Command and the US Strategic Air Command. Could the Americans have gone alone without taking the UK with it?

Macmillan considered the consequences of the note from his intelligence chief so important that he immediately sent a copy to the Queen.

There is little doubt that the events of those tense days took their toll on the British politicians at the centre of events. Defence Minister Peter Thorneycroft recalled an unreal, almost sinister, tranquillity as he crossed St. James's Park on the Sunday of that fateful weekend. Whitehall was deserted. It was very quiet, but rather a beautiful autumn morning. As he approached the Ministry of Defence he remembered thinking, 'My God, I wonder whether this really is it.'

Nerves were equally taut at a meeting at Admiralty House later that morning, as Macmillan, Butler, Home, Thorneycroft and Heath awaited news of Khrushchev's reaction to Kennedy's letter. When the Soviet response came through, the Prime Minister received the news in a state of exhaustion. He had been up throughout the

Friday and Saturday nights, aware that the world stood on the brink of nuclear conflict. Macmillan himself recalled his feelings – that relief and gratitude came 'almost with a sense of anti-climax, after days during which it was difficult to restrain, yet necessary to conceal our emotions ... We had been on the brink, almost over it ...'

It was as a result of Macmillan contemplating the events of that tense October that he ordered a post-Cuba rethink of War-Book planning to make sure the system worked faster and more appropriately. Within a few hours of Khrushchev agreeing to pull his missiles out of Cuba, the Chiefs of Staff in the UK and Peter Thorneycroft, Minister of Defence, realised how the events had exposed devastating weaknesses in Britain's plans. The Cabinet Secretary, Sir Burke Trend, wrote a memorandum to Thorneycroft in which he said, 'After the Cuba crisis the Prime Minister directed that the Home Defence Committee should review the state of the Government War-Book planning in order to ensure that it was sufficiently flexible to enable us to react quickly and appropriately to a sudden emergency in which we might have no more than two or three days' warning of the outbreak of war.' And the Joint Intelligence Committee prepared a special study of how mis-calculation could so easily lead to nuclear war.

All of this took place out of the public's gaze. Perhaps it was as well that the people of Britain did not appreciate how close they had been to unthinkable nuclear confrontation. The public would have been panicked had they known that the national 'evacuation plan', designed to disperse some 19.5 million people from nineteen major cities expected to be prime targets, was never considered or activated, as the missile crisis reached its most tense period.

There were some very positive outcomes of the crisis. Most importantly for the safety of the world, one was the creation of the Hot Line, a direct communications link between Moscow and Washington to allow the leaders of West and East to talk directly to each other in any future crisis. The events of October 1962 illustrated starkly the appalling consequences of one false decision, or one fatal misunderstanding. The leaders of the two super-powers learned that lesson from those thirteen days on the brink of the world's most frightening conflict. For Moscow and Washington, and for Britain too, it marked the end of a tense period of Cold War nuclear brinkmanship. Within twelve months the world's two super-powers made three significant arms-control agreements. The Hot Line was set up in June 1963. In August the same year a nuclear test ban treaty was signed by the United States, the Soviet Union and Great Britain. Finally, the crisis led to talks that eventually resulted in 1969 in a treaty on the non-proliferation of nuclear weapons. The Cold War dragged on, dominating lives across the world. There were periodic incidents when tensions mounted. On each side, technology generated weapons that were more sophisticated, more frightening and more accurate. But, thank goodness, in the three decades of Cold War that remained, the world never again approached so close to that ultimate threshold which could have destroyed mankind.

Shortly after the Cuban crisis *The Times* published a letter, signed by forty-two leading Labour politicians. It said:

> *If Russian missiles in Cuba were a threat to American cities (as we believe they were) then United States missiles ringing the USSR are equally a threat to Soviet cities. This is the lesson that millions have learnt from the terrifying events of the Cuban crisis. Now that Mr Khrushchev has withdrawn his missiles, Mr Kennedy should respond similarly. Unless the West makes some counter-concession, Mr Khrushchev's present policies may be replaced by tougher ones. We in Britain should press the United Kingdom Government to ask Mr Kennedy to remove his Polaris and Thor missile bases from our country immediately.*
>
> *These bases heighten world tension. They also make it certain that the British people would be incinerated in the first hours of a world war.*

It was a forceful plea. But apparently unknown to Opposition politicians the decision had already been made. Thor was a stop-gap weapon. It had been a sabre that was rattled effectively during the crisis. But in the USA new, more efficient intercontinental missiles were poised in their bunkers. Thor was becoming obsolete. Despite a rearguard action by Air Marshal Sir Kenneth Cross and some other military leaders, the politicians had concluded that the future of Britain's nuclear deterrent lay elsewhere.

It was too vulnerable. There was no possibility of concealing it in underground silos, and in any case the intercontinental missile was now in front-line use in the United States. America had no need any longer of a defensive missile fence this side of the Atlantic.

CHAPTER 15

Thor Disbanded

Many people, including some of the former Thor crew-members, believe that the Thor missiles were withdrawn from the UK in 1963 as part of the same covert deal that Kennedy struck with Khrushchev over the Jupiter missiles in Turkey and Italy. They were not. The ironic fact is that when the Cuban missile crisis broke, the imminent disbandment of the RAF's Thor squadrons had already been decided.

The original agreement between the US and UK governments to deploy Thor in the UK stipulated a five-year period. In 1961 the Vice-Chief of the Air Staff put forward arguments for extending the deployment, and there was lengthy discussion in the Air Council over a period of months before a firm decision was taken in May 1962. This spelt the end of the RAF's venture into IRBM squadrons. The run-down was to begin in the spring of 1963 and be completed by the end of that year. Before that, however, Thor had its moment of history. In the eyes of those closest, involved at the launch sites, October 1962 proved its worth as a deterrent. The announcement of Thor's demise, as far as the RAF was concerned, was slipped out almost casually by Peter Thorneycroft, then Minister of Defence. On 1 August 1962, in answer to a question by an Opposition MP, he announced its gradual withdrawal. Thorneycroft gave the Commons more details in December that year, when he said that the 4,000 men in the Thor force would be released for other duties, and the run-down would represent a saving in maintenance costs of £1 million a year. He added that there was a possibility that Hemswell and Driffield would be retained on a care-and-maintenance basis. New units would be drafted in to Feltwell and North Luffenham, but there would be no further RAF use for all the satellite stations that had housed launch emplacements for forty-eight other missiles.

The initial public statement to Parliament, two months before Cuba, obviously signalled British intentions to the Soviet Union. Perhaps it also carried a false message that the UK ballistic missile squadrons were no longer the threat they had been. The Russian authorities would have been wrong to jump to that conclusion. But the fact that he knew Thor's days were clearly numbered could be the reason that Khrushchev ignored their menace when it came to making demands for the removal of the less-effective, and potentially less-threatening Jupiter missiles in Turkey and Italy.

Writing to Sir Kenneth Cross, AOC Bomber Command, on 2 August 1962, the Air Minister, Hugh Fraser, explained, 'The Government's decision to bring to an end, during the course of next year, the arrangements under which Thor missiles are stationed in this country, foreshadows the close of a memorable chapter in the history of Bomber Command.'

His letter continued: 'Thor was the first strategic ballistic missile system deployed in the free world. You may well be proud that you pioneered the introduction of these weapons into military use. The high state of readiness at which the Thor force has been maintained, the record of serviceability sustained, and the success achieved with Combat Training Launches, reflects the greatest credit on all concerned.'

The following day, hiding his own personal disagreements at the decision to disband the force, Air Marshal Cross issued an order-of-the-day to all Thor squadrons:

The decision to phase out the Thor Force of Bomber Command in no way detracts from the vital role which the force played in the past, and the significant part it will continue to play in the future, until the very last missile is withdrawn.

Thor was the first strategic missile system operational in the West. At a time when the threat to this country came almost entirely from manned aircraft, you were the most formidable part of the defence of the United Kingdom, and the Western Alliance.

You in the Thor Force have maintained a constant vigil day and night for almost four years. You have maintained a higher state of readiness in peacetime than has ever been achieved before in the history of the armed forces of the Crown. I am well aware of the sacrifices, so willingly accepted, that this constant readiness has imposed on the officers and airmen of the force.

I am content that history will recognise your devoted service in the cause of peace. I know that I can rely on you for the same devotion during the run-down phase as you have shown since the birth of the force in 1958.

Gp Capt Kenneth Pugh, who commanded the Driffield group of Thor bases, said the announcement by the Government to disband the missile squadrons was a heavy blow to everyone concerned. 'Everyone had been so dedicated to the Thor force we just couldn't believe it', he said.

Later in August, the 7th Air Division of the USAF was informed that the run-down would commence on 1 April 1963. The force would run down operationally by the end of September that year, and it was hoped that the shipment of all missiles, warheads and technical equipment back to the United States would have been completed by the end of 1963. During the phase-out period the RAF would maintain a shrinking operational capability and combat training launches would stop immediately.

Despite the tension that stretched across all the Thor squadrons during the Cuban crisis alert, in the middle of it, at the end of October 1962, a detailed phase-out plan spelling out what must happen at each launch site as the run-down programme got under-way, was issued by Bomber Command. Launch crews could be forgiven for thinking they were living in an 'Alice in Wonderland' world: at one moment preparing for the worst, even perhaps nuclear annihilation; at the next planning their own demise!

When the end for the Thor squadrons came, many in the Thor force were keen to get back to flying duties. Most of the officers and senior NCOs who made up the Thor launch-crews were air-crew. Others, particularly those in the technical trades, had seen the missile era as the future. They were getting in on the ground floor of a new era for the RAF by gaining experience with Thor. At that time there was an expectation that the UK would develop its own medium-range missile, Blue Streak. But the demise of Thor marked the end of the short strategic missile era in the service. Many were pleased to move on to flying duties. But some looked back on the Thor period with fondness and favour. Len Townend, who as one of the training experts at Feltwell, where the RAF Missile School had been established, says: 'Thor was the most interesting and most satisfying job I ever had in the RAF.'

A test dismantling operation took place at one of the launch emplacements at Breighton, the base for No. 240 Squadron, in December 1962. The squadron's Operational Record Book notes that on 20 December at 13.00 hrs launch emplacement No. 40 ceased to exist – the dismantling having taken thirteen days.

Throughout 1963 the closing-down of the twenty Thor squadrons proceeded, complex by complex. Driffield and its satellite bases was the first wing to close, followed by Hemswell, Feltwell, and finally North Luffenham. The Operational Record of the North Luffenham Wing recorded that Nos 144, 130, 218, 223 and 254 Squadrons became non-operational on 15 August 1963, and were disbanded on 23 August. On that date the Thor era in the RAF officially ended.

Marshal of the Royal Air Force Sir Thomas Pike, Chief of the Air Staff, wrote:

> *The high morale which was a feature of the Force from its inception has never flagged, and Thor's fine record of serviceability and state of readiness over the years is a remarkable tribute to the loyalty and sense of duty of all personnel who played a part. They will be able to look back with pride on a most valuable contribution to our deterrent force.*

Six years later, the UK's main strategic nuclear deterrent reverted to ballistic missiles, this time carried by submarines. In June 1969, responsibility for the UK's nuclear deterrent transferred from the RAF to the Royal Navy, with the introduction of Polaris. The previous year, Bomber Command had been disbanded with a ceremonial parade and a flypast by representatives of the three bombers of the V-force – the Vulcan, Victor and Valiant. The only two Thor missiles that still remain on this side of the Atlantic, forty-five years after the most dangerous period of the Cold War, are in the RAF Museum at Cosforth, and at the National Space Museum at Leicester. The missile at Cosforth is a former training round used by the RAF, and the rocket on display in the Space Museum is a Thor Able of the type used in the USA during the space exploration programme. Together, they are lone memorials to the Thor force and the four thousand men who served in it.

CHAPTER 16

A Story of Firsts

I t was the end of the Thor launch sites in England, but it was not the end of Thor. The rocket went on to become the workhorse of America's emerging space programme. Thor played a vital role in the development of America's reconnaissance satellites. It was crucial to the Midas programme, which launched an early-warning satellite capable of detecting the heat surge of an incoming Soviet intercontinental missile. Similarly, it was the vehicle that launched America's first camera-eye satellite, the development that took over from spy-planes like the U2 and made the risks of manned intelligence-gathering over-flights of Soviet territory a thing of the past. Thor was the first rocket to boost a payload into polar orbit of the Earth, and it formed the first-stage vehicle for unmanned reconnaissance of the Moon, the lunar probe pro-gramme. In doing so it was the first man-made object to escape the Earth's gravitational pull. Thor logged over 500 successful flights as a mainstay of NASA's space programmes. As the Commander of the US Air Research and Development Command, General Bernard Schriever, the man who was responsible for driving through the development of America's ballistic missile programme, commented, 'The story of Thor is the story of achievement, a story of firsts.'

A group captain who was in charge of one of the complexes of launch bases, asked years later how he felt, being involved with so

179

much destructive potential, with fifteen missiles capable of more destructive power than the total bomb-loads of all the bomber sorties from Lincolnshire bases in the Second World War under his charge, said it was difficult to analyse his feelings, the warheads looked so innocuous.

> I was helped [he said] by a small incident fairly early in my command. I was at one of the satellite stations on a cold foggy morning. I went into one of the Thor shelters which were kept at a temperature of about 70 degrees Fahrenheit. There was no one else present and above the noise of the air conditioners I could hear the sound of a bird singing cheerfully. I saw this small sparrow perched on the warhead fluffing out his feathers. He was happily enjoying himself away from the miserable conditions outside. It was nature's way (or God's) of giving me a sense of proportion. The bird had got his priorities right!

Thor Technical Specifications

Length: 65 ft
Diameter: 8 ft
Weight: 110,000 lb (fuelled)
Fuel: Rocket-grade RP-1 (kerosene)
Oxidiser: Liquid oxygen
Propulsion: A single combustion chamber from an MB-1 or MB-3 engine generating 150,000 lb thrust
Two Vernier engines, each generating 1,000 lb thrust
Range: 1,500 miles
Guidance: All-inertial
Accuracy: Two miles
Re-entry vehicle: Mark 2
Warhead: W-49, 1.44 megaton yield
Contractors:
  Airframe: Douglas Aircraft, Santa Monica, California
  Propulsion: Rocketdyne Division of North American Aviation, Canoga Park, California
  Guidance: AC Spark Plug Division, General Motors, Detroit, Michigan
  Re-entry vehicle: General Electric, Saratoga, New York

The Thor Squadrons

Station	Duration	Squadron	Commanding Officer	Duration
Cambridgeshire:				
Mepal	22/7/59 to 10/7/63	No. 113 (SM)	Sqn Ldr P.J. Hearne	Jul 59 to Feb 62
			Sqn Ldr P.S. Cockman	Feb 62 to Jul 63
East Yorkshire:				
Driffield	1/8/59 to 18/4/63	No. 98 (SM)	Sqn Ldr P. Coulson	Nov 59 to May 61
			Sqn Ldr S. Hudson	Jun 61 to Jun 63
Carnaby	1/8/59 to 9/4/63	No. 150 (SM)	Sqn Ldr E.R. Haines	Aug 59 to Feb 60
			Sqn Ldr D. Downs	Mar 60 to Sep 61
			Sqn Ldr R. Milton	Sep 61 to Apr 63
Catfoss	1/8/59 to 9/3/63	No. 226 (SM)	Sqn Ldr E. Morriss	Nov 59 to May 61
			Sqn Ldr P. Hart	Jun 61 to Jan 63
Breighton	1/8/59 to 8/1/63	No. 240 (SM)	Sqn Ldr R.W. Steel	Aug 59 to Jul 61
			Sqn Ldr L. Hacke	Jul 61 to Jan 63

Station	Duration	Squadron	Commanding Officer	Duration
Full Sutton	1/8/59 to 27/4/63	No. 102 (SM)	Sqn Ldr L. Baldchin	Nov 59 to Dec 61
			Sqn Ldr J. Slater	Jan 62 to Apr 63
Folkingham	1/12/59 to 23/8/63	No. 223 (SM)	Sqn Ldr F. Lister	Feb 60 to Nov 61
			Sqn Ldr C. Bruce	Nov 61 to Aug 63
Leicestershire:				
Melton Mowbray	1/12/59 to 23/8/63	No. 254 (SM)	Sqn Ldr D. Liddle	Dec 59 to Aug 61
			Sqn Ldr E. Beer	Aug 61 to Nov 61
			Sqn Ldr D. Bailey	Nov 61 to Feb 63
Lincolnshire:				
Hemswell	1/12/59 to 24/5/63	No. 97 (SM)	Sqn Ldr R. Tate	Jul 59 to Feb 61
			Sqn Ldr R.K. Collyer	Mar 61 to May 63
Caistor	22/7/59 to 24/5/63	No. 269 (SM)	Sqn Ldr T.A. Dicks	Sep 59 to Jun 61
			Sqn Ldr P. Edelsten	Jun 61 to May 63
Bardney	22/7/59 to 24/5/63	No. 106 (SM)	Sqn Ldr R.F. Keatley	Jul 59 to Feb 62
			Sqn Ldr T.C. Woods	Feb 62 to May 63
Ludford Magna	22/7/59 to 24/5/63	No. 104 (SM)	Sqn Ldr D.H. Young	Jul 59 to Dec 60
			Sqn Ldr B. Bourne	Jan 61 to May 63
Coleby Grange	22/7/59 to 24/5/63	No. 142 (SM)	Sqn Ldr W.A. Gill	Sep 59 to Mar 61
			Sqn Ldr J. Abrey	Mar 61 to Apr 63
			Sqn Ldr E. Dodds	Apr 63 to May 63
Norfolk:				
Feltwell	1/9/58 to 10/7/63	No. 77 (SM)	Sqn Ldr S.O. Baldock	Sep 58 to Nov 61
			Sqn Ldr K. Hayes	Sep 61 to Jul 63
North Pickenham	22/7/59 to 10/7/63	No. 220 (SM)	Sqn Ldr F.R Leatherdale	Jul 59 to Feb 62
			Sqn Ldr R. Henderson	Feb 62 to Jul 63

Station	Duration	Squadron	Commanding Officer	Duration
Northamptonshire:				
Polebrook	1/12/59 to 23/8/63	No. 130 (SM)	Sqn Ldr W. Hibbert	Dec 59 to Feb 60
			Sqn Ldr D. Lister	Feb 60 to Aug 61
			Sqn Ldr H. Millar	Sep 61 to Aug 63
Harrington	1/12/59 to 23/8/63	No. 218 (SM)	Sqn Ldr J. Burch	Dec 59 to Nov 61
			Sqn Ldr F. Slaughter	Dec 61 to Aug 63
Rutland:				
North Luffenham	1/12/59 to 23/8/63	No. 144 (SM)	Sqn Ldr W. Hibbert	Feb 60-Nov 61
			Sqn Ldr R. Hale	Nov 61 to Aug 63
Suffolk:				
Tuddenham	22/7/59 to 10/7/63	No. 107 (SM)	Sqn Ldr P.P. Flood	Sep 59 to Jan 61
			Sqn Ldr H.G. Norton	Feb 61 to Jul 63
Shepherd's Grove	22/7/59 to 10/7/63	No. 82 (SM)	Sqn Ldr B.J. Knight	Jul 59 to Dec 60
			Sqn Ldr R. Lingard	Jan 61 to Sep 61
			Sqn Ldr W.A. Young	Oct 61 to Jul 63

Bibliography

Boyne, Walter J., *History of the US Air Force 1947–1997*

Cockcroft, Wayne D., and Thomas, Roger J.C., *Cold War: Building for Nuclear Confrontation 1946–1989*, English Heritage

Cowley, Robert, *The Cold War*

Duke, Simon, *US Defence Bases in the United Kingdom: A Matter for Joint Decision?*, Macmillan Press

Gaddis, John Lewis, *The Cold War*, Allen Lane

Gaddis, John Lewis, *We Now Know: Rethinking Cold War History*, Oxford University Press

Hartt, Julian, *The Mighty Thor Missile in Readiness*, Duell, Sloan and Pearce

Hennessy, Peter, *The Prime Minister: The Office and its Holders since 1945*, Allen Lane

Horne, Alistair, *Macmillan 1957–1986*

Menaul, Stewart, *Countdown: Britain's Strategic Nuclear Forces*, Robert Hale

Proceedings of the RAFHS Seminar on the RAF and Nuclear Weapons, 1960–1998', *Royal Air Force Historical Society Journal*, 26

Reed, Thomas C., *At the Abyss – An Insider's History of the Cold War*, Random House Publishing

Reeves, Richard, *President Kennedy, Profile of Power*

Sagan, Scott D., *The Limits of Safety: Organisations, Accidents and Nuclear Weapons*, Princeton University Press

To Defend and Deter: The Legacy of the United States Cold War Missile Program, US Department of Defense

Twigge, Stephen, *Anglo-American Air Force Collaboration and the Cuban Missile Crisis: A British Perspective*

Twigge, Stephen, and Scott, Len, *Planning Armageddon – Britain, the US and the Command of Western Nuclear Forces 1945–64*

Twigge, Stephen, and Scott, Len, 'The Other Missiles of October: The Thor IRBMs and the Cuban Missile Crisis', *Electronic Journal of International History*

Twigge, Stephen, and Scott, Len, *Fail Deadly? Britain and the Command and Control of Nuclear Forces 1945–64*, Aberystwyth

Wood, Derek, *Attack Warning Red – The Royal Observer Corps 1925–1992*, Carmichael and Sweet

Wynn, Humphrey, *RAF Strategic Nuclear Deterrent Forces: their origins, roles and deployment 1946–1969*, HMSO

Index